This book was Video-taped in 1996 by the Steven Spielberg Shoa Foundation.
It is called
A copy can be found in Museum in Jerusalem.

A cassette tape of the exp... was commissioned in 1997 by the London Imperial War Museum, specifically for the new extension to the museum, opening in the Year 2000.

A copy of this book can also be found in the British Library and the Stationers Hall Registry, 1999.

"Please, do not allow the Holocaust to remain
a footnote in history.
Please, teach this in your schools,
Please, listen to the words,
The echoes, and the ghosts."

Steven Spielberg

© Copyright No. 3115711
Published by Claire Parker,
14 Netherhall Gardens, London NW3 5DQ

All rights reserved, by any form, or any means, for the publisher.
Printed by Elmar Printers, London N18 3PN.

I would like to support and highly recommend this book by Clare Parker. It is an excellent example of trying to describe the indescribable, in a way that will have meaning for those who read it. Clare's primary concern is to make these accounts of atrocity accessible to children, and thereby educate them about the dangers of facism and totalitarian regimes. It is important for Clare, who lost her own childhood - in the Holocaust, that future generations of children should not have to suffer the same fate.

Judith Hassan
Director of Services for Holocaust Survivors,
Refugees and Families, Jewish Care

Introduction

What follows is a documentary. Facts. History.

As an eye-witness I believe it is my duty to tell all that I experienced, on behalf of the vanished millions who cannot speak.

These people did not fight a civil war.

They did not die on a battlefield.

They were not part of any conflict.

They were hunted down, city by city, country by country.

They were systematically murdered.

There is no comparison in history.

My story will be brief, as short as I can make it. With every page, every line, every word, I shall give you my recollection of the events as they happened in what remains for me the very recent past.

Klara

1
Schooldays.

We are going back in time to the year 1942. We are in Pesterzsebet, a suburb of Budapest, the capital of Hungary. My name is Klara. I am not yet eleven years old.

I go to the elementary school nearby. Our teachers are very strict. We are not allowed to talk in class except to answer a question from the teacher. We must sit straight up, hands behind our backs, palms against the back of the desk bench. There are forty of us in the class. There are two rows of desks, two pupils to each desk. There is a big cross on the wall and a cane on the teacher's desk. Should any one of us fail to keep absolutely still, he or she is immediately punished. A girl gets whacked a few times on the palms of her hands with the cane. A boy has to bend over to receive several strokes on his backside.

My school is a big elementary state school, not a religious one, but Hungary is a Catholic country so the children are all Catholics. Except for me. Even though I am the only Jewish child in my class, no-one knows I am in any way different until one day when the teacher announces that a priest is coming to give religious instruction to the class age six. I am to go and stand in the corridor for one hour. It is a very cold winter. There is deep snow everywhere. The heating in the school only comes from the wood-burning stoves in the classrooms so it is no warmer in the hall than it is outside. There is nothing for me to do but stand shivering by the window in total silence, looking at the snow.

Discipline is strict and even in the playground we have to be on our best behaviour. But from this day on the children keep taunting me with shouts of 'dirty four-eyes Jew' (I wear glasses). Although I am very hurt and upset, I never speak of this at home.

We are at school from 8 a.m. to 12 noon. Then we have a lot of homework to do. Television has not yet been invented. Children learn handicrafts, they sew, they read books. I draw

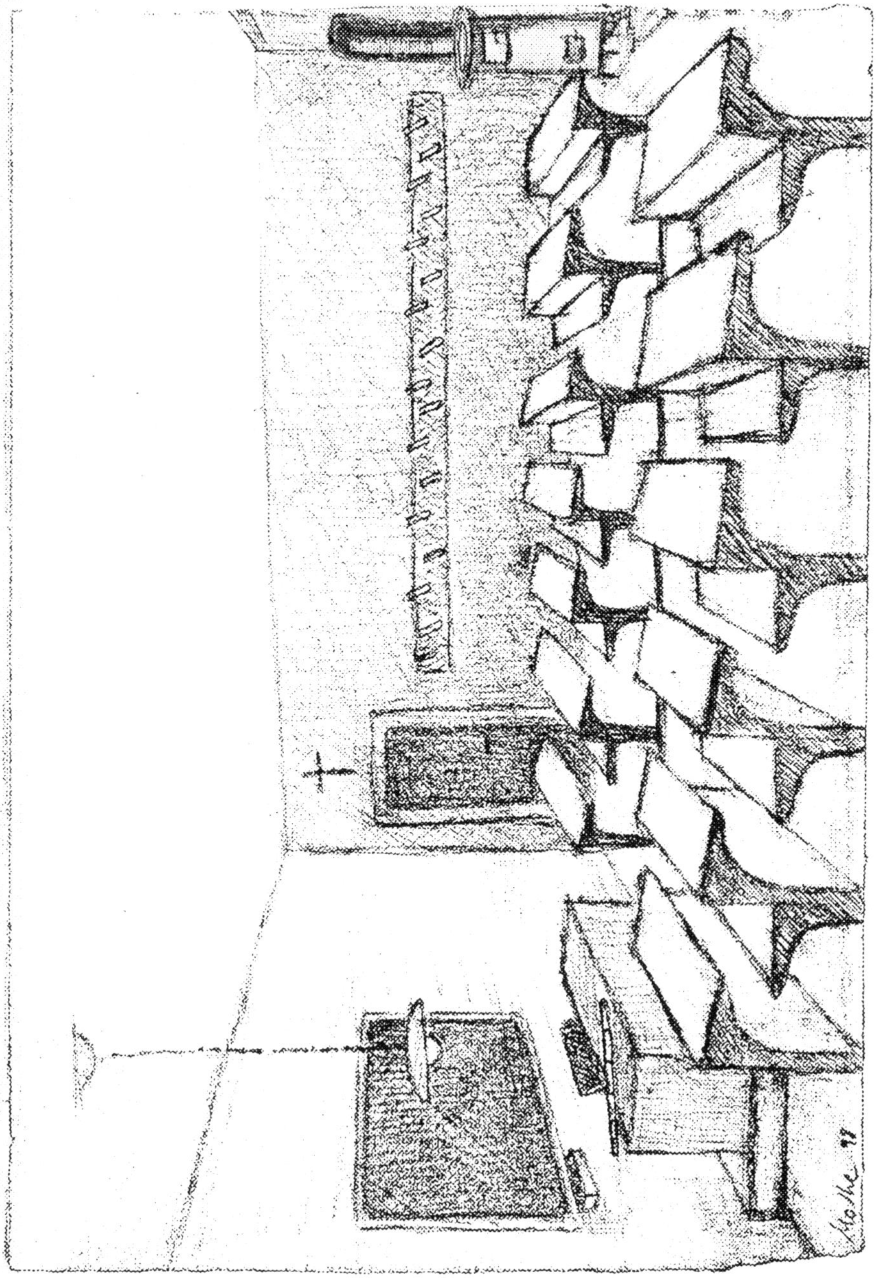

dresses and coats, I learn embroidery, I keep busy. I dream of the future, of becoming a fashion designer.

Once a week, after school, I go to the synagogue study-room where I learn the Hebrew alphabet. In those days, we only learnt enough to read the prayer books. Hebrew was not taught as a language to converse in. But we were told that our forefathers spoke Hebrew in ancient Israel. We were taught that all Jews originally come from there and that we must learn the history of our ancestors and the language of prayers.

When the time comes to move up one class at this state school, forms have to be filled with many details, including nationality and religion. The teacher brings back the form I have handed in and tells me that since I am Jewish I cannot be Hungarian. She has crossed out 'Hungarian' and replaced it with 'Israelite'.

The fact that I am refused the nationality of my birth because of my religion does not immediately strike me. My first reaction is to exclaim:

"Oh, how do you know about Israel? I thought only Jews learnt..."

"Quiet!" she snaps,"don't talk when you're not questioned!"

When I get home that day, I do relate the incident although I am too young to understand that it is a sign of things to come.

Our Courtyard: Top Centre: My Father's workroom, his car & bicycle. We lived to the left in the illustration

2
Family Life

I am now eleven years old, an only child. My mother sews. She makes clothes for the whole family. My father has a metal-plating workshop in the courtyard which we share with two other families. All the flats are on the ground floor. Another girl lives there, eight months older than I am. She goes to a religious Catholic school and each family keeps very much to itself, so we do not know each other very well.

All the members of my father's family live about two hundred kilometres away, in a small town with a big name: Hodmezovasharhely! We can only visit them in the Summer, but one of my father's brothers often comes to see us.

My mother's relatives live in and around our suburb, not far from one another. Most Sundays, we go and visit my maternal grandmother and so do the rest of the family. There are quite a lot of us and her living-room is big enough to accommodate us all. My grandmother has a housekeeper who bears the same name as herself, Margit. Margit, always in her big white apron, was already there before I was born. She is like an aunty to me.

Whenever the family have troubling discussions about the war now raging in Europe they do not want me to listen to them, so I am sent to help Margit in the kitchen. When, occasionally, my parents go to the theatre, I spend the night at my grandmother's and it is Margit who takes me to school in the morning. Sometimes I also stay with my uncle, my mother's brother, and his wife. I love their three-and-a-half year old daughter, my little cousin Eva.

My parents could not take me to most restaurants and places of entertainment because children were not allowed there. But I remember going to one restaurant where we sat in a lovely big room which looked to me like the dining room in a palace, with Gipsy musicians and singers. Children aged ten and over were tolerated only if they could stick to the rules: speak in a very quiet voice and never leave the table without an adult. There were girls selling small bunches of flowers from a basket and a waiter would bring vases to keep them in. The leader of the Gipsy band would come to the table to ask what you wished to hear and they would play your request.

My father owned a nice, big car for his business so in the Summer we were able to drive to some picturesque old inns on the banks of the Danube, where tables were laid out of doors. I remember the way they used to cook freshly caught carps in a huge copper pot suspended over an open fire, making a fish-goulash, a delicious local stew which we ate with freshly baked rolls. We would enjoy the view of the river as boats floated by. And almost always, wherever food was served, there was lively Gipsy music.

Until my problems started at school, I led a happy, carefree life.

3
Secrets and Whispers

Then came 1943. The second world war had been raging in Europe for over three years.

By law, we had to camouflage all windows and doors every night so that no light could show through and present a target to flying aircraft. Every evening, after doors and windows were tightly closed, we would turn on the radio and tune in to the B.B.C. World Service giving us truthful news of the war in our own language. Listening to the London news was strictly forbidden and only a pro-Nazi version of the events was to be heard daily on Hungarian news. We were always hoping to hear that the Germans were losing the war. Hitler's anti-Jewish propaganda was gaining ground in Hungary as elsewhere and Jews were beginning to lose their jobs. The BBC World Service was a life-line for the Jewish people. But for how long?

I was warned not to talk to anyone about listening to the English news and the discussions that followed or we could all go to prison, or worse. I had learnt the 'Hatikva', a Hebrew song of hope which was later to become the Israeli national anthem. I was told not to sing it outside our home.

The children at school had become so horrible to me that I was afraid to go to school. But I still told no-one at home.

One day, the young girl I vaguely knew in our courtyard told me that if I could keep a secret she would take me to see a church. I had never been inside a church so, intrigued as any child would be, I followed her. When we got there, she asked me to look at the statues. On the way home, she said:

"Did you see that man on the cross? He is our God. The Jews killed him".

I was speechless with shock. I had to go home and ask my parents who had killed this man. I had never heard the story before, so I believed that it had just happened and that my parents might know who had committed the crime! It was explained to me that this had taken place in the land of Israel 2000 years ago, that Jesus was a Jew executed by the Romans who had invaded our homeland which was renamed Palestine,

Our old wooden radio - called "The Wireless"

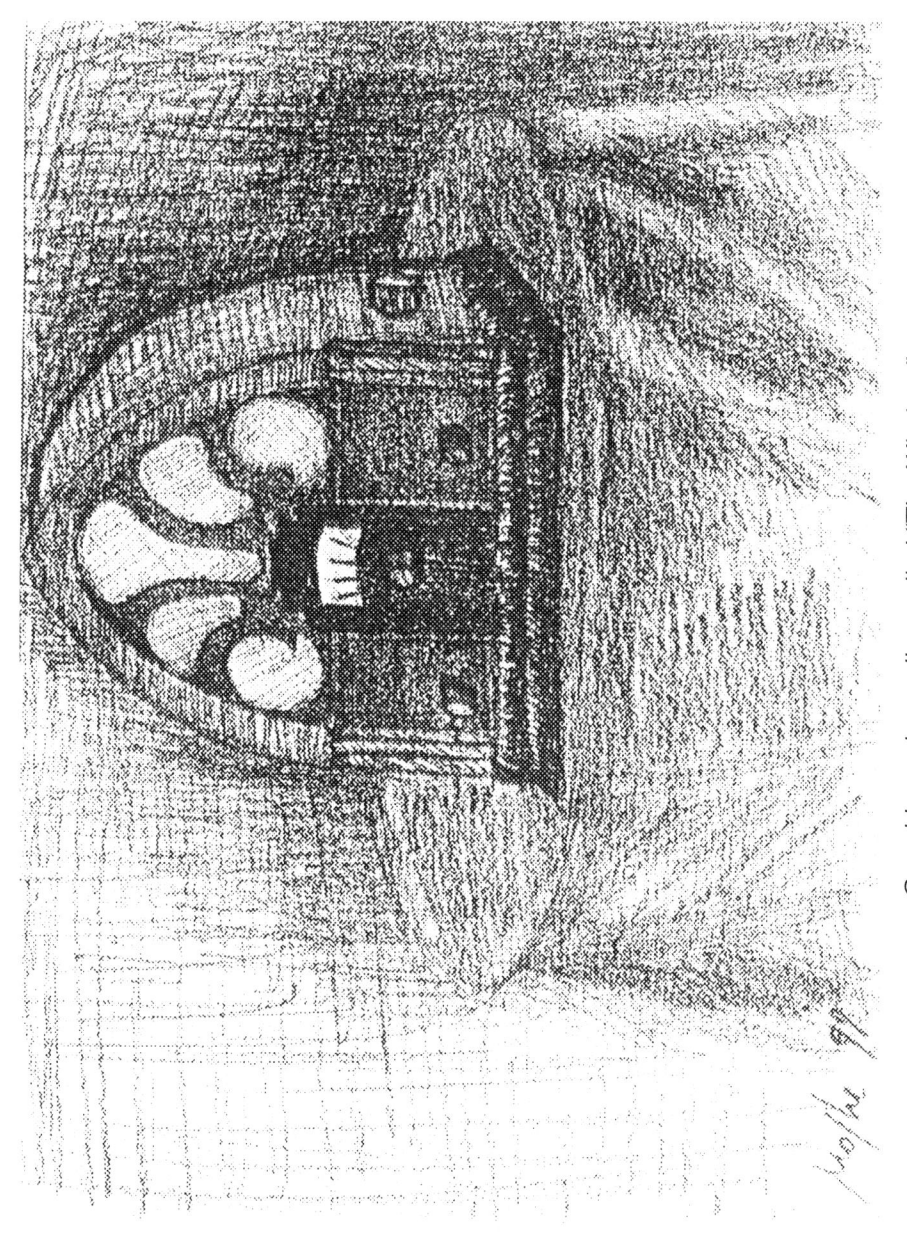

and so on... Once again, I was warned to keep all this to myself, not to try and answer any accusations as it would only lead to more trouble.

I began to hear repeated whispers within the family about Palestine and possible ways to get there. Although travel abroad was not forbidden as such, it was impossible for us to obtain the necessary travel documents. Now, whenever I stayed with my grandmother, it was to enable my parents to attend meetings where they were trying to plan an escape from Hungary.

With my Parents
Age 6/7, Pesterzsebet, Hungary

4
Living in Fear

Then the situation worsened rapidly. There was no point in having meetings any more as it became clear that leaving Hungary undetected with old people and children would be quite impossible. Trying to plan an escape was pointless.

Suddenly, all Jewish men between the ages of 16 and 60 were sent into forced labour camps under the guise of work for the war effort. My father was sent to a place called Katzko in the Carpathian mountains where a forced-labour group worked in the forest as lumbermen for a wood factory. Although at first he was able to come home for a few days now and again, his workshop had to be shut down. My mother could not drive the car or run the workshop and in any case my father did not want her to do this kind of work. As it turned out, all Jewish businesses were soon to be closed down anyway.

By then I was really scared of going to school. One day, on my way home after class, no longer content with shouting insults, the children pelted me with stones. I was only slightly hurt physically, but upset and frightened and even though they had not known of the previous harassment, my family decided that I should stop going to school.

We tried a private teacher, a Jewish lady. But she lived in another suburb and travel was difficult. Winter comes early in Hungary; the days are very short and the streets are dark. So this was to be the end of my schooling. I was eleven-and-a-half years old.

For non-Jews, life went on as usual in spite of the war. Walking along the main street one evening, we saw young people getting out of their cars, girls in long evening dresses, men in dinner jackets and bow-ties. We could hear the music of the dinner-and-dance they were going to attend, by the popular composer Franz Lehar. From the street, we could see the glittering colours of the ballroom through the first floor windows.

Most Jews, having lived in Hungary for many generations, still trusted the Hungarian people. In family discussions, I would hear comments to the effect that Hungarians were not as anti-

This is one of the live broadcasts we heard on the Hungarian News – A street scrubbing event that Jews were forced to carry out in Vienna

Semitic as Germans, Austrians and Poles, that Hungary would never maltreat its Jews as the others did... Yet the situation was getting worse. I could only catch snatches of conversations, I never heard anything in detail, but the word 'ghetto' was often mentioned. When I asked the meaning of the word, my parents' answer was,

"We don't know ourselves. The stories we hear are too hard to believe."

My father came home on one of his short visits. Playing in the yard under one of our windows, I overheard a conversation between my parents . My father was saying:

"I have been offered to convert to Catholicism; in return I would no longer have to do forced-labour."

After some exchanges on the subject, he told my mother,

"I cannot do this. What would happen to everyone else in the family? If the others have to die, I would rather die , too."

How was a child to react to such talk? Although there was much I could not understand, the continuous atmosphere of impending danger and the constant need for secrecy affected me deeply. Because everyone around me felt threatened, so did I.

5
More repressions

For a while after this incident, I cannot be sure of the dates or even of the order in which events followed. As far as general occurrences are concerned, memories of a time lived in fear and apprehension tend to blur into one another somewhat, especially when you are too young to fully comprehend the situation. I remember posters beginning to appear on shop windows and places of entertainment with the caption: 'Jews and dogs forbidden'. There was a corner shop nearby where I, like other children, used to buy sweets. From one day to the next I could no longer go there. Why? I could not understand and I was terribly hurt.

My grandmother had a talk with Margit, the housekeeper, advising her to go and work in a safer household. Margit understood the situation, but she explained that having no family of her own, she considered us as her family and she wanted to stay and help us. She could do the shopping safely since she was a Catholic. She remained with us until we were forced into a ghetto.

A farmer offered to hide my mother if things got worse. She begged him to take me and her mother as well, trying to convince him that we could all help on the farm. When he said that he could only hide one person, my mother refused the offer, just as my father had refused to convert long before we knew that it would have made no difference anyway.

The radio news from London was always optimistic, always full of hope of an imminent German defeat, but Margit would bring us the local Hungarian rumours. The Germans had invaded a number of countries where the Nazis were now in control. And they were marching on.

In Hungary, new laws were being passed all the time to make Jewish lives more difficult. It became almost impossible to visit relatives as we were allowed out only two hours a day and the order came to wear a big yellow star on our clothes when out in the street to make us more easily identifiable.

1943
Sent home
No more school for Jewish Children

1943
The Yellow Star
- Jews allowed on the streets for
only 2 hours per day

6
Nazi Hungary

It was 1944. The radio news from London still kept our hopes up as the allies, the Russians on one side, the British on the other, were closing in on the Germans, so the war should end soon...

Meanwhile, we heard through the Hungarian Radio News that Admiral Horthy, Hungary's head of state, was acting like a king and that new pageantry was being introduced, such as the changing of the guards. Horthy was described leading the ceremony astride a white horse, medals sparkling in the sun, followed by the troops in a variety of flashy uniforms, with a new 'special guard' on horseback, the 'chendors'. We were soon to find out what these new guards were meant to do. Also in the parade was Cardinal Minsenty, the head of the Hungarian Catholic church, in his white and gold finery. It was he and Horthy together who took the decision to make the Nazis welcome in Hungary. So was Hungarian history and the shameful part it played in the Holocaust made by these two men.

From then on, not only sanctions but atrocities against the Jews escalated rapidly. The news that reached us were horrendous: Jews were being lined up on the banks of the Danube and shot dead into the river; others were made to dig their own graves at gunpoint and then shot into them. A few were kept alive long enough to throw some earth over the bodies, then it was their turn to be murdered. Every minute of what should have been ordinary, everyday life became terrifying for us.

The German army poured in, long columns of soldiers, some on high tanks, some on motorcycles with side-cars, arms stretched out in front of them in the nazi salute, swastikas and the letters SS prominently displayed on their uniforms. Our flat was on a main road and I clearly remember watching all this, the swastikas on the flags and the SS lettering on the helmets which were to become a symbol of all our fears, of all the persecutions we were to suffer.

Then came the order, on the Hungarian radio news, that a new greeting, 'Better Future', ('Szeb Jovot' in Hungarian) was to replace 'Good Morning' or 'Hello'. Catching snatches of conversation, I understood it to mean that once Hungary was rid of all its Jews, life would improve, there would be more of everything and at cheaper prices. And the Hungarian people believed it. It is amazing how gullible people are, how easily they can be brainwashed into accepting a scapegoat.

Soon, Horthy gave the order that all Jews living in Budapest's inner city were to move into houses especially marked with the yellow star. This was to be the ghetto. But we lived in the suburbs, so our family didn't have to move.

7
Legalised Looting

I was now twelve years old. Staying home from school, I was cut off from other children, alone with my mother who spent most of her time writing letters to the whole family because our telephone had been disconnected.

One day, as the two of us were sitting at the table having our lunch, there was a commotion outside. We heard horses hooves approaching, then stopping in the yard. A chair outside our door was knocked over. The door, which was unlocked, was thrown open violently as two men burst in. They were the new guards with feathers on their helmets, the chendors. I could see more of them in the yard and their horses tied to a tree. One of the two men inside pointed his gun at us, demanding the rings and necklaces we were wearing while the other one was throwing into a box any valuable objects he could find: candelabra, trays, a copper mortar and pestle. A big box holding documents had been chrome-plated by my father. Thinking it was silver, they tipped out all the papers and took that as well.

They carried their loot outside and came back in, opening every cupboard, every drawer, tearing quilts and pillows, demanding to know where we kept our jewellery. Then, with their bayonets, they ripped open the lining of our coats because the word had got around that persecuted Jews were trying to save some valuables by hiding them in whatever they might be able to carry with them.

When, having found nothing, the two of them went back out, the ordeal was not over yet. Two others came in and demanded 'all the paintings'. We only had two, but they kept asking,

"Where are the others?" looking under beds, behind wardrobes, everywhere.

They were so filled with the Nazi propaganda which told them that all Jews were wealthy, that they would not accept what their own eyes told them, that there was nothing else of value to take. When finally they all left, I remained numb with terror and shock.

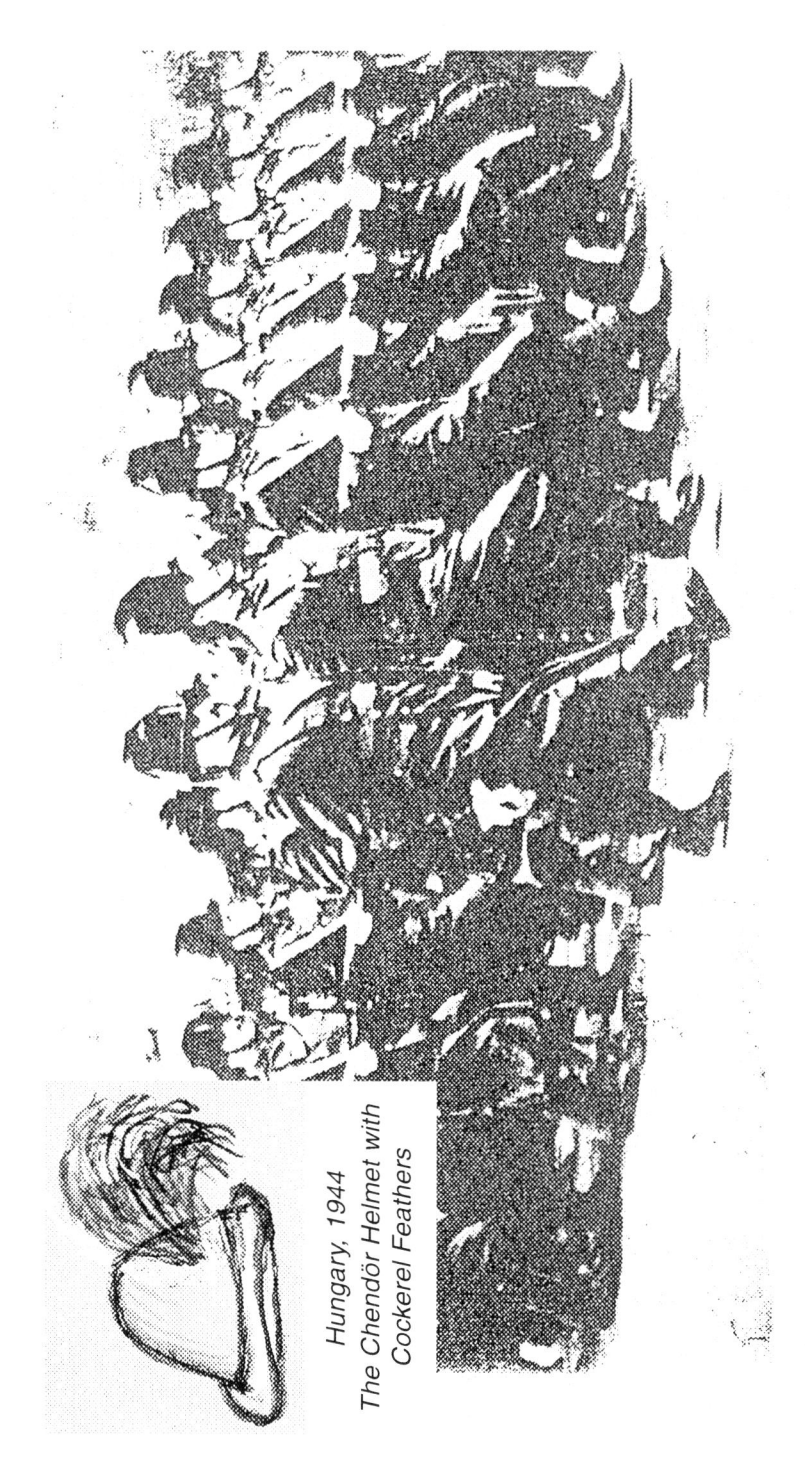

Hungary, 1944
The Chendör Helmet with Cockerel Feathers

The Hungarian Gendarmerie, which after the German occupation of Hungary on March 19, 1944, became the major instrument of state power in the ghettoization and deportation of approximately 440,000 Jews.

Every detail of that episode will remain clear in my memory for as long as I live. It was the first time that I was directly threatened by uniformed men with guns, and in the name of the government.

Soon after this, Margit came to see us with news of my grandmother. The same thing had happened to her. Her cherished leather-bound books had been taken, but she was sending with Margit the gold bracelet I had left behind the last time I had stayed at her house. She had hidden it in her apron pocket and the chendors had missed it.

A few days later my father managed to come and see us for a few hours. He was taking a chance and must not be missed. In spite of everything, he was still optimistic and felt that the end of the war was near.

It was not long before the chendors were back again, this time for my father's car. They did not even ask for the key hanging inside the house. They must have had one of their own and just drove the car away. They also opened up the shed and helped themselves to my father's bicycle.

I had been brought up never to take anything that did not belong to me. When visiting relatives, if I wanted a piece of cake or a sweet or even a glass of water I had to ask "may I ?" I kept asking myself how anyone could behave the way those men did and get away with it. I thought of my father who had told us of working twelve hours a day from the age of fourteen, sleeping in hostels and eating little and cheaply in order to save enough to start a small workshop in a basement. This became both his workplace and his home for several years, until he felt that he had saved enough to ask my mother to marry him. I felt that having worked so hard for what he had, he surely did not deserve to lose it all.

Father's Car - He used it to collect and return work

8
The Ghetto

Out of the blue, the order came to leave our flat. It was our turn to move into the ghetto, a small area where thousands of Jews would be crammed together. Most of our belongings had to be abandoned as we were to share a tiny place with my grandmother. We had one room, a kitchen and a larder. No toilet. No water. I had never before seen an outhouse in a garden in lieu of toilet. Clean water had to be brought in from a neighbour's garden tap. Dirty water had to be poured out into the garden. The neighbours had three children, including a fourteen year old girl, Susan. When I discovered that at last there was someone closer to my age to whom I could talk, I went to fetch water constantly as an excuse to meet her.

Our one room could only accommodate one double bed which my mother, my grandmother and I had to share. The few pieces of furniture we had tried to salvage and brought with us were stacked up to the ceiling, unusable for lack of space.

The kitchen had a wood burning stove for which wood had to be bought from shops that we were not allowed to enter. Yet we managed to get enough wood to do the cooking. In spite of the posters which forbade the Christians to sell to the Jews, there was a thriving black market. One corner grocery store owner was risking his licence by selling us food secretly at the back of his store at exorbitant prices.

My mother and my grandmother were often crying. We knew nothing of our other relatives and did not find any of them in the ghetto. We supposed that maybe, because they lived in other parts of town, they had been sent somewhere else.

From a Hungarian Newspaper Cutting 55 Years ago in 1944, in the middle of the night, we were rounded up from the Ghettos. The special guard clearly visible on the right

9
The Railway Lines

One morning, before daybreak, we were ordered out of bed. We could hear the chendors' horses and orders being shouted in the streets. We were to leave everything behind, pack only one bag or suitcase each, and go and gather in the middle of the road. We were then marched in an orderly column five abreast. There were only women there, apart from very young boys and very old men. All able-bodied men had now been working in slave-labour camps for some time.

The bags were heavy, people having taken with them as much of their belongings as they could possibly carry. We had to walk on and on, street after street. It was still dark . There was no-one else about, no traffic at all. We were not allowed to talk. We had no idea where we were going. There were little children among us, but even they were very quiet. We were all too shocked to make a sound.

It is a terrible, frightening time, when freedom is no more and laws are made no longer to protect you but to persecute you. I could never have imagined then that worse was yet to come.

As dawn was breaking, we reached some vast empty grounds around a derelict brick factory. This was apparently our destination for now. Everyone collapsed on the ground to rest. After a short while, we all began to look for relatives among the thousands brought here, its suburbs and greater suburbs. We found my grandmother's other grandchild, my little cousin Eva, now four years old, and her mother. We gathered up four bricks for a makeshift stove. We had brought with us whatever provisions we had at home and were able to prepare something to eat.

There was a tap by the roadside and I volunteered to fetch water. But at the sight and sound of German soldiers barking out orders to Hungarian soldiers, I was frightened and returned to my mother. The water tap was near some railway lines and I asked about the railway. Everyone else seemed to have guessed or maybe they knew more than I did. When the place

On the way to a brick factory, then on to Auschwitz

was functioning, bricks were being made here and then transported somewhere else by rail. Now we were here, apparently also to be transported...

We remained there for three days and nights in terrible conditions, many thousands of us living on the ground in the open, sitting on our belongings, guarded by heavily armed Hungarian and German soldiers. At some point, the very old and mothers with very small children were separated from the rest and sent under the cover of a huge shed, a sort of roof on poles, not a proper building.

When the little food we had taken with us ran out, we began to starve.

I understood from conversations between my mother and my grandmother that we now had no home left anywhere, because in Hungary most homes and business premises were not owned, but rented. When rent payments stopped, the landlords would repossess the premises and appropriate their contents.

Then the wagons arrived. I understand that tourists now visit what is left of these railway lines. They cannot possibly begin to understand the horror of it all, they cannot picture the conditions, both physical and mental of the people being shoved into cattle wagons by heavily armed soldiers screaming at them in a language they do not understand. I did not know where we were going, I did not know what would happen to us, I did not know why any of it was happening at all.

This is where I heard for the first time the shouts of "Schnell! Schnell!", German for "Hurry, Faster" which were going to be a constant accompaniment to every outrage committed against us in the months to come. With thousands of women and small children having to squeeze hurriedly into the overcrowded wagons, there was no room for all the luggage as well. The bulk of those last few possessions had to be left behind.

The one wagon – close up

10
Destination Unknown

We sat on the floor of a high cattle wagon, huddled against one another, having been ordered to leave an empty space in the middle. The wagons seemed to me nothing but dirty , big wooden boxes on wheels. High up on either side of the locked doors, four small windows with metal bars instead of glass let in a little light.

With us were two armed Hungarian soldiers. Besides some canvas bags, they had three wooden boxes which they used, so as to make themselves comfortable in the cleared central space, as a table and two seats on which they spread some blankets. Then they began to bark orders at us:

"Quiet! No talking! Keep the centre clear! And from now on, no moving about."

There was no room to move anyway. There were some children with us, but the very young and the very old who had been taken under cover were missing. We found out later that they were in separate wagons.

We started to roll. I was unable to judge how long the journey lasted. One at a time we stood up for a minute, our backs to the soldiers. When my turn came, I tried to see through the barred windows but they were too high. I still had no idea of where we might be going. Most people were weeping, silently wiping their tears. Not a whimper could be heard.

Sitting on their boxes, the two soldiers were talking and laughing, their guns protruding conspicuously from their belts. They took out food from their bags, spread it on the makeshift table between them and started to eat and drink from a bottle, water or wine, I don't know. We had been without any food for days and we stared at their picnic. We watched them cut off the crust from the bread and drop it into a paper bag to throw it away. My stomach was in knots.

The train had stopped from time to time. Now it came to a complete standstill. Ordering us to stay put, the two soldiers got off. Then we saw German soldiers, heard harsh, shouting German voices. They made us get down from the wagons but ordered us to remain alongside the train. Some people could understand their commands and translated them into Hungarian for us all. We were forced to leave any remaining possessions by the side of the wagons.

There were thousands of people, hungry, frightened, in shock. Some were still at a loss to understand what was happening to them, others realised that the rumours they had heard, too horrendous to be believed, were turning out to be true, but no-one really knew exactly what would happen next.

We had arrived at Auschwitz, Hitler's main extermination camp.

A train arriving at Auschwitz, 1944
Hungarian jews are still locked inside

11
First Selection

I was to learn many years later that between April 7th and June 11th, 1944 , all the Jews of Hungary, all 433,000 of them, were sent there. This was Auschwitz in all its horror, not the place that visitors see now. No-one looking at the empty grounds fifty years later can imagine what I lived through as a child. And yet I am one of the very few lucky ones, since I am here to tell the tale.

Among the many thousands were many like my own family, decent, hard-working, honest human-beings, minding their own business, living life as best they knew how. For many of them this was the last day of their lives. Others would take a little longer to die. Very few would survive. Those of us who did have to bear for the rest of our lives the nightmare of our memories and the irrational guilt feeling of not having died with our loved ones. Time cannot erase or even dim any of the details of the events imprinted on my mind so indelibly that if I close my eyes, they seem to be happening now. And the horror and the pain are too intense to be expressed in words.

As I stand by the wagons, I watch the high-ranking SS men in their shiny boots and smart uniforms, guns on their shoulders and at their belts, each carrying a stick or a whip under one arm. They ask those of us who can speak German to come forward and they choose some interpreters from among them to translate into Hungarian their orders, their questions and our answers.

First we are told to take nothing with us, to drop right where we are whatever we may still be carrying. There is smoke in the air, a light grey smoke and with it a strange smell I cannot recognise. Then we are told to walk forward in a single file. This is the last time we are recognisable as human beings...

I am tall for my age and used to being mistaken for older than I am. As we move forward, someone (my grandmother? my mother?) whispers anxiously, close to my ear:

"Say that you're thirteen years old".

The Polish jews arrived before us. They were helping, clearing away our belongings. We had to form a line 5 x 5, to be selected by Mengele. All under age 12 and over 50 vanished that day.

The huge crowd keeps moving forward. As one by one we answer questions, some of us are directed to the left, some to the right. My grandmother is in front of me. She is sent to the right. We cannot say good-bye. I will never see her again. She is fifty-three years old.

I am next. I give my age as thirteen although I am only twelve. I am sent to the left. My mother is behind me. She is sent to the left as well. This ritual is conducted with the constant accompaniment of German soldiers and SS men barking "Schnell! Schnell!" as they press the crowds forward. We are walking between two rows of electrified fences.

For those who are marched to the right, children twelve and under and adults over fifty, this is the end. They will be sent to the 'shower' room, but what will come out of the shower heads will not be water but a lethal gas. Then there will be the crematorium and the grey smoke...

But of course I knew nothing of that then. Many things were incomprehensible to me at the time. I was also to find out many years later that the high ranking SS man who made those decisions of life or death for each of us as we walked past him was the terrible Dr Mengele who performed experimental surgery without anaesthetic on children when he did not send them to die in the gas chambers outright.

Because I lied about my age , I am the youngest survivor of this side of the Auschwitz concentration camp. On the other side of the railway line was what is known as Auschwitz-Birkenau, a slave labour camp where you worked until you dropped. But here, we were in the extermination camp. For those who were sent to the right, death was immediate. The others would have to wait their turn and maybe be put to work in the meantime, there were too many to deal with at once.

12
The Nazi Machine

By now, jostled both by the crowd and the men with the guns, I have lost sight of my mother. I don't know where she is. I am alone in the crowd. There are so many women... There are many women among the SS too, in uniform, but apparently without guns and whips, at least none that I can see.

We are hustled into a huge, poorly-lit room. Above our heads, pipes are running, criss-crossing in all directions, with shower-heads at every junction. Those of us who wear glasses have to place them on a long table against the wall. We must take all our clothes off and pile them under the table. There are soldiers everywhere and we are standing naked. Because of the crowding we cannot see what is happening ahead of us. We have to wait. We are standing under the showers, but no water comes.

Then we see what is happening. Some women prisoners who were here before us, with numbers tattooed on their forearms, are shaving our hair, head and body. Most of us are also branded with a number. It is explained to us that only those who look strong enough to be put to work need a number. The rest, like myself, will go ...somewhere else. And with a laugh:

"It is only a matter of time. There are too many of you here".

By this time, everyone understood what was happening: no number meant that you were to die sooner; you were not going out of this camp alive, not even for slave labour. It was a German woman in army uniform who was explaining this and laughing. She was as inhuman as the men.

When the shaving and branding was over, we were all pushed and shoved out again, one by one, naked and hairless, humiliated, dehumanised, between two rows of glaring SS men and women. You could tell from their uniforms that there were very high ranking officers as well as ordinary soldiers. As we walked between the two rows of staring faces, we were being sprayed from top to toe with some kind of disinfectant. We stayed without anything on until one dress each (no underwear) was handed out to us from a pile of rags, no doubt the worst of those left by other prisoners. We tried to cover ourselves as fast as we could but of course nothing fitted anybody; some dresses were too small to get into, others as big as shrouds. We tried to swap. Some of us still had our shoes on - I had mine - others had to try and find some.

We then stood, five abreast in an endless file. The younger girls, from thirteen to sixteen, were sorted out from the rest and everyone was allocated barracks numbers. I was to go with all the teenagers into C lager, barracks 12.

All through this I could not see my mother anywhere.

13
Searching for Mother

The lager was a long alley like a street, but unpaved, with sixteen numbered barracks on either side, even numbers on one side, uneven ones on the other. The barracks were just long, high wooden sheds with very high tiny windows at the top for ventilation.

It was fairly dark inside but we could see the rows of wooden bunks, 3 tiers in height, 2 bunks in depth, each bunk just a large platform on which twelve of us would have to lie together. There was nothing else, no bedding of any kind. The place was empty besides those built-in bunks.

Some of us tried to find somewhere to sit down, others walked about trying to find someone they knew, a few tried to look through the little window of a small cabin inside the shed, near the entrance.

I noticed two young women with proper clothes on and hair on their heads. It would turn out that the cabin was their quarters and that they, too, were prisoners, but chosen to be the spokesmen between whoever gave the orders and the rest of us. You could say that they acted as supervisors. Somehow, maybe from them, information was soon being passed around that there were two washroom barracks halfway down one side of the C lager and toilets at the other end, even though there were no signs to be seen anywhere. In fact, I had not even seen a sign saying 'Auschwitz'. All that could be seen on arrival was the name of 'Birkenau' on a plaque at ground level, on the other side of the gate, indicating the direction of the slave-labour camp. I never saw the infamous gate that everyone has come to know with the ironic words "Arbeit Macht Frei" (Work Liberates You) because it was at the entrance to Auschwitz-Birkenau , the slave-labour side of the Auschwitz concentration camp.

I had to find my mother. Determined to look into every barracks, I zig-zagged from one side of the lager to the other, starting at number one. All the barracks had their doors open, all were unbelievably crowded with women. There was no crying, just talking in low voices. I was not crying either. But I was going inside every doorway shouting "Mummy! Mummy!" at the top of my voice. In one of the barracks, someone grabbed my shoulder. It was one of my aunts. How could I have known her? Head shaved and in rags, everyone looked the same. She was shaking me and saying:

"Stop this! Most of us here are mothers. If you want to find yours, you have to call her name. But calm down!"

I know I wasn't crying, but I must have sounded hysterical because she kept repeating:

"Stop it! Stop it!"

But of course she was right about calling a name. So I went on from barracks to barracks, shouting "Mummy, Mrs Hochhauser!" at each one, two or three times, then waiting a little. Nothing happened. Eventually, I tried the washrooms. They were empty. I kept on going and shouting, still not crying. But some women looked at me and covered their faces to hide their tears.

I went on searching for a long time. After the thirty-two barracks and the washrooms there was nowhere left to look except the toilets. This was my last hope. So I went in there.

It was just another barracks, but without the bunks. Instead, I saw this row of holes and people sitting, standing, talking. It seemed that at this moment the toilets were not being used as such but as a meeting place. By now I was desperate, shaking uncontrollably and crying and shouting "Mummy, Mrs Hochhauser!" And as I was standing there in tears my mother grabbed hold of me. She had been sitting right there; we had not recognised each other. We were both crying, so were other women around us, everyone asking or thinking the same thing: "What has happened to us? What have we been reduced to?"

Two supervisors came, telling us to leave the toilets and go into our barracks. I remained with my mother and never went back with the teenagers.

The toilet Barracks, where I found my mother Hundreds of women, dressed in their one piece of rag and with their heads freshly shaven It was a terrible sight to behold, within hours of arrival Auschwitz C Lager

The wooden barracks are no longer there, but this picture shows the way it was then We had nothing but only the bare wood to sleep on, no blankets over us to keep us warm

EMPTY BARRACKS: 500,000 people visit the worst Nazi death camp annually

14
The Camp

All the barracks were the same, long wooden sheds, light coming in as if reluctantly from high, narrow openings under the roof. The crowding on the three tiers, two deep bunks was such that we had to lie one up, one down, like sardines in a tin, for everyone to be able to get in. On these bare wooden boards, in such crowded conditions, even sleep was difficult and painful.

In the small cabin inside each barracks lived the supervisors responsible for forwarding the orders of the camp commanders. They were also meant to be our interpreters but we were all Hungarian and they were Polish. I never found out how long they had been there, if their hair had never been cut off or if it had grown out again. They wore proper clothes. Theirs seemed somewhat privileged conditions compared to ours. I don't know how we communicated with them or they with us. They must have been chosen because they knew some German and no doubt some people on our side did too as students in Hungarian schools had to study German from the age of eleven . Somehow the orders always came through.

From time to time, we were allowed to come and go within the lager, to the washroom and toilet barracks. From the outside, these looked just like the other sheds. But the toilet barracks were fitted with long wooden boxed-in platforms bearing a double row of holes one next to the other. The washrooms consisted of endless rows of cold-water taps set along a pipe above what looked like an interminable metal trough with holes all along for the water to run off. We could drink out of our gathered hands, but to wash ourselves was another story.

The soil of the lager, of beaten earth, was hard as stone as there was no rain for the time that I remained there. But beyond the washroom back doors the ground was all mud. There was not a blade of grass to be seen, nothing growing anywhere. On either side of the C lager ran high electrified barbed-wire fences curving inward at the top. Close to these fences were those of

the adjoining lagers, their tops curving the other way. So contact was impossible from one lager to another.

15
Life in the Camp

A routine of sorts was adhered to. At night, both the front and the back doors of our barracks were closed. I don't know if they were locked. I never found out because we had so little to eat or drink that I never needed to get up at night. In the morning, the supervisors would open the front doors wide, but never the back ones, to allow us to go to the washrooms and toilets.

The SS men, bayonets at the ready, conducted endless roll-calls. We stood there, five abreast in one long file on either side of the lager between the barracks. We would stand for hours on end, until they would decide to start checking us out. This useless exercise was repeated several times a day. At first, when there were one thousand women in each barracks, the standing and waiting on one spot seemed to last all day, a torture in itself.

At what may have been lunchtime, a cupful of grey liquid was served up from what looked like giant metal garbage bins. And always, walking among us, were the SS men with their bayonets, handguns and whips, shouting, always shouting, barking orders and insults. To this day, hearing the German language, even spoken quietly, makes me shudder...

Occasionally, after standing for some hours for the roll-call, we were allowed to sit on the ground, then we stood again for the second and last meal of the day which was handed out by the soldiers. This consisted sometimes of one very thin slice of something unrecognisable shaped like salami, and at other times one slice of a paste, a liver-pate look-alike, either of them without bread. When, occasionally, we each received one slice of a strange looking bread, there would be nothing else to eat with it.

The officers and high-ranking SS never did anything. They walked about in their highly polished knee-high boots, whip in their gloved hands, watching us. We never looked at them, much too afraid to catch their eyes. The last thing we wanted was to bring ourselves to their notice. I learnt never to look at them, careful to keep my eyes to the ground at all times.

Worst of all were the 'selections' of which we had a taste on arrival. Every few days at first, gradually more often and eventually every day, the barracks would be emptied two at a time and their inmates taken through the selection process. This was more or less a repetition of what had taken place on the day of arrival. We would have to strip naked and leave our rags in a pile. Then came the spraying from head to toe with disinfectant and that terrible walk between two rows of SS men and officers until a high ranking SS, usually the dreaded Mengele, chose who should turn to the left, who to the right, one by one.

And every time, those who were sent to the right were never seen again.

I went through so many of these dreaded selections that I soon lost count. Those who, like myself again and again, were directed to the left, were given some other rags to put on and sent back to the barracks where we had to remain until the supervisors allowed us out again to the toilets and washrooms. After each selection, the orders of the German command to the supervisors were to keep us inside for several hours. It is during that time that the ones who had been 'selected' to go to the right vanished without a trace.

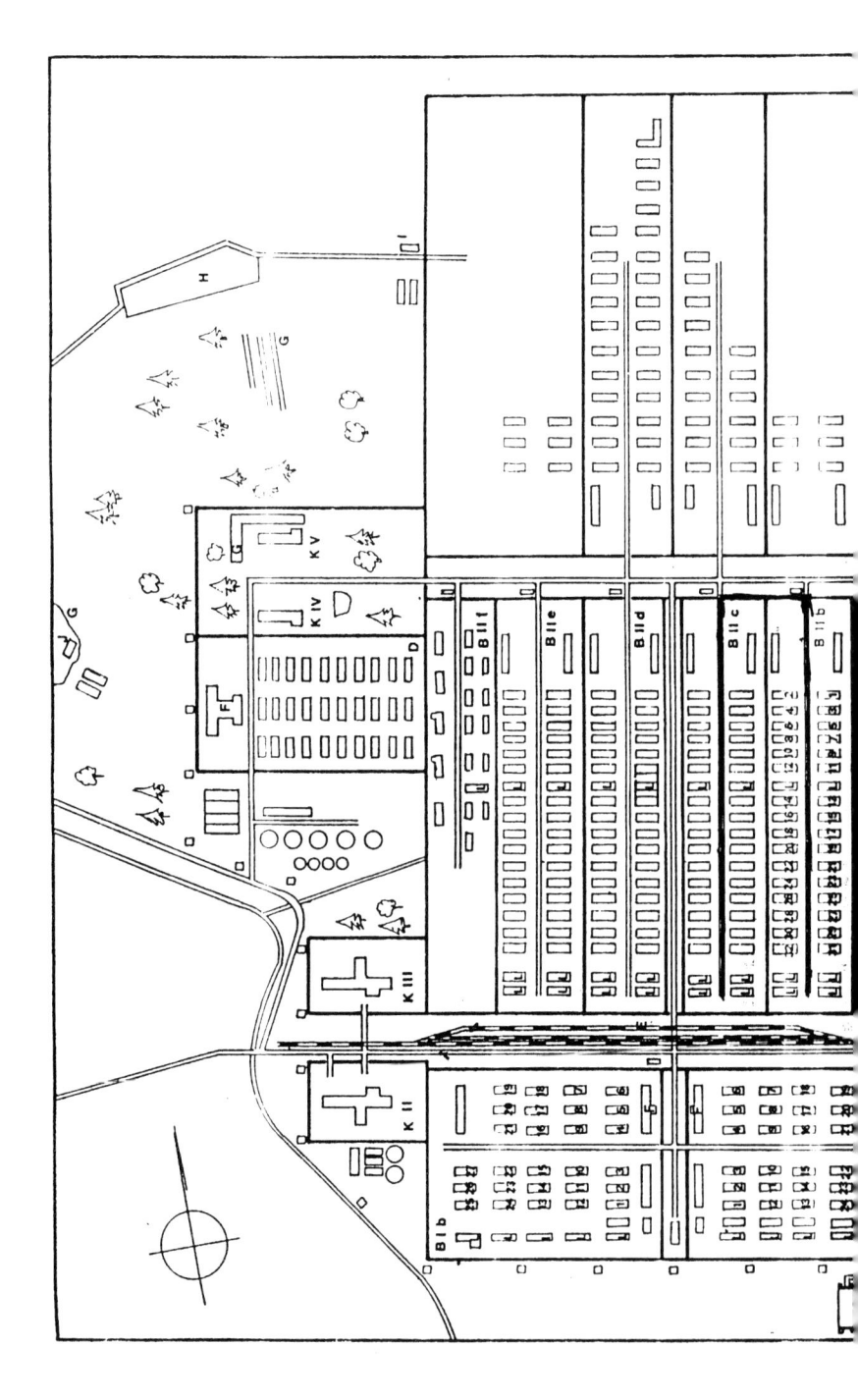

C. Lager, for Hungarian Women

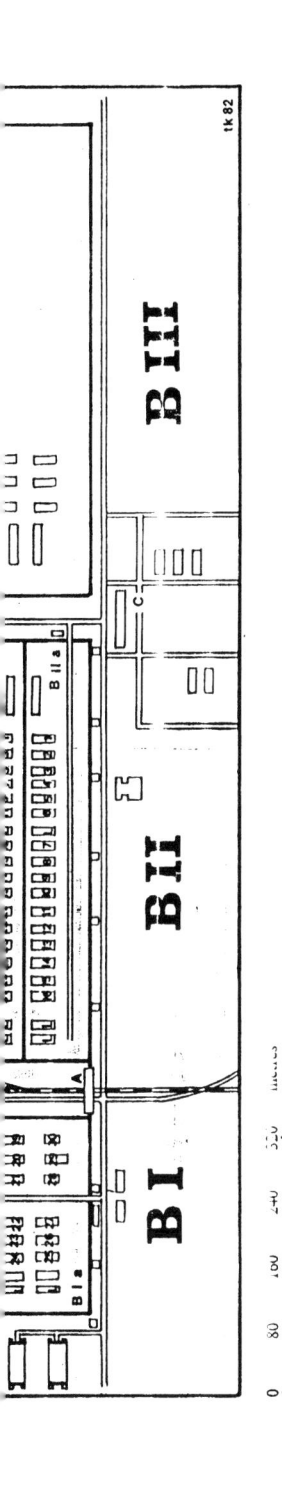

Map of Auschwitz II-Birkenau (corresponding to the aerial view shown in photo 8)

- A Main gate and guardhouse
- BI Sector I
- BII Sector II
- BIII Sector III ('Mexico'), under construction
- BIa Camp for women
- BIb Initially a camp for men; from 1943, a camp for women
- BIIa Quarantine area
- BIIb Family camp for Jews from Theresienstadt
- BIIc Camp for Jews from Hungary
- BIId Camp for men
- BIIe Camp for Gypsies
- BIIf Holding area for sick prisoners ('Infirmary')
- C Camp headquarters and SS barracks
- D 'Canada', the area of warehouses used for processing belongings plundered from deportees
- E Ramp where Jews were subjected to selection for the gas chambers as they descended from the trains
- F Showers ('Sauna')
- G Pits and open areas where corpses were burned
- H Mass graves of Soviet prisoners of war
- I First improvised gas chamber (the 'red house')
- J Second improvised gas chamber (the 'white house')
- KII Gas Chamber and Crematorium II
- KIII Gas Chamber and Crematorium III
- KIV Gas Chamber and Crematorium IV
- KV Gas Chamber and Crematorium V
- L Latrines and washrooms

Note: The system of numbering prisoners' barracks in compounds BIIc, BIId, and BIIe was the same as that in compound BIIb.

[53]

46

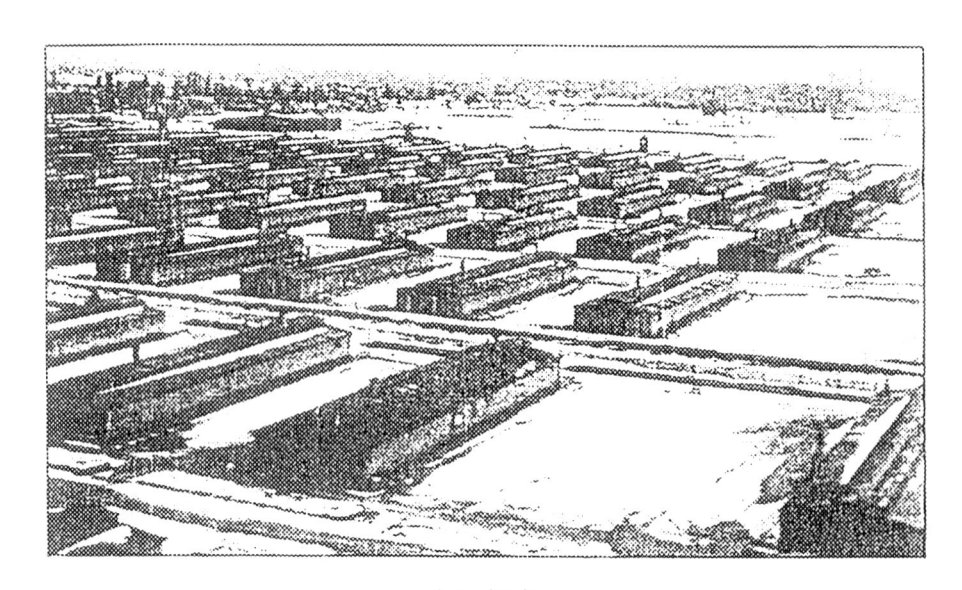

Auschwitz
The Lagers with wooden barracks

Auschwitz
Interior of the wooden barracks

16
Countdown

Time was meaningless. We had no idea of hours, days, months. As there were less and less women left, some joined us from other barracks and one shed after another became empty. As the process speeded up and selections took place almost daily, there were more empty barracks, less women left. I did not know where they went to. As far as I was concerned, they just vanished. I was a child and I still could not fully understand what was happening. I did not question the constant smoke hanging over the camp as in those days wood and coal were used for heating and cooking and made a lot of smoke and all these soldiers and officers lived there.

It was many years later, long after the war was over that I found out the meaning of the shower-heads which when switched on gave not water but murderous gas, and of the grey smoke with the strange smell: who was considered unsuitable for work too old or too young or too weak - went straight to the gas-chambers and then the crematoria. Only a few of those who disappeared were occasionally selected to leave the Auschwitz extermination camp for a forced-labour camp. Looking back, I think that all the women around me knew what was going on while we were shut up in the barracks after each selection, but they shielded me from the truth.

There were no pregnant women among us. Those who had not been found out at the first selection were discovered eventually and sent to the right...

As the thousands of women I had arrived with gradually vanished, not only were some barracks emptied out, but the time came when there was much more room to sleep, just a few of us on each bunk, mostly on the middle tier.

Running along the length of the barracks between the two rows of bunks was a brick wall one metre high, half a metre wide. Now and then an SS officer would stride along the top of this wall, shouting in German, making threatening gestures with his baton. We stood frozen, each one hoping that she would not be one of those he managed to hit. After such a performance, one of us would usually warn the others in Hungarian to do whatever had been commanded, whatever the two supervisors would tell us to do as they would pass these orders down, or else!

I remember the pace of the nerve-wracking selections speeding up and the number of women dwindling until only two barracks of the C lager were occupied out of the thirty-two, one on either side of the washrooms. We could see the B lager through the two sets of electric fencing between us and the situation there was the same. Only a few women remained.

17
Last Selection

The seasons were changing and with only one flimsy rag on for all clothing we began to feel the cold badly . At the same time, many changes occurred very rapidly. The roll-calls stopped. Suddenly none of the supervisors, the Polish women in charge in every barracks, were anywhere to be seen. They, too, had vanished. So the spray session and rags exchange of the selection for the last two barracks was directed by three SS, two women and one man .

I had survived dozens of selections. This was to be my last one. I was twelve and a half years old.

We came out of the barracks on either side of the washrooms to form one single line that went through the grisly routine: take off rags, stand to be sprayed with disinfectant on one side, turn around to be sprayed on the other side, walk naked between the two human walls, only two metres apart, formed by the staring SS top-brass.

This time, at the end of the routine, I was directed to the right. I picked up a rag and walked towards the barracks on the right. By the time I dared turn around, I could not see my mother. As there were many SS around at selection time, we could only do as we were told, so I went inside. I could not see outside because the doors were swinging closed after each woman went in.

There were not many of us now. I looked at all the bunks on both sides: my mother was not there. Everybody sat, waiting. Gradually the noise abated outside. No more women came in. The last selection was over. All the women in the barracks on the left would now be kept strictly indoors while the barracks I was in was emptied out and its occupants who had been sent to the right, including myself, would be made to "vanish".

As I mentioned before, we never used any of the back doors which were close to the electrified fence. I had never tried to find out whether or not they were locked. I tried to collect my thoughts. "I am in this barracks, then there are the washrooms,

51

then the other barracks where my mother must be. I have to find her."

It does not even enter my mind that I have been condemned to die. All I know is that once again I have been separated from my mother and once again I have to do anything in my power to find her.

I stand near the back doors. After a while, all sounds from outside have stopped completely.

My heart is pounding at the thought of trying out the back doors. My thoughts are racing. " There is no-one around the back, only on the front of the buildings. And even there, where the supervisors used to go in and out at night to meet one another, leaving the doors open, there was no-one else to be seen. Now even they have gone."

I give a gentle push on the back door. It swings open. Even though I was hoping it would open , I did not really expect it to so I am somewhat taken aback. I venture a few steps. All hell breaks loose. Ear-splitting sounds rent the air, whistles blow, dogs bark, voices shout. I forgot about the watch-towers!

I run along the back of the washroom barracks. One of my shoes sticks in a very soft muddy patch. I step out of the shoe, see the back door open and run in. In front of me are stored a large number of those huge dustbin-looking containers from which food is served. I jump into one and pull the lid over my head. At the same moment, I hear a German voice shouting just outside,

" Come on out or I'll shoot."

There are words you hear so often that they no longer need to be translated.

Dogs are barking close by.

From under the warped edge of the bashed lid, I can see moving lights. It is not yet dark outside , but it is very dim inside here. I guess they are using torchlight. I can hear containers being kicked. The mud is too soft to keep footmarks and my abandoned shoe points alongside the barracks; they cannot tell from it which direction I followed before hiding. Finally, there is complete silence. But I am too terrified to come out of my hiding place.

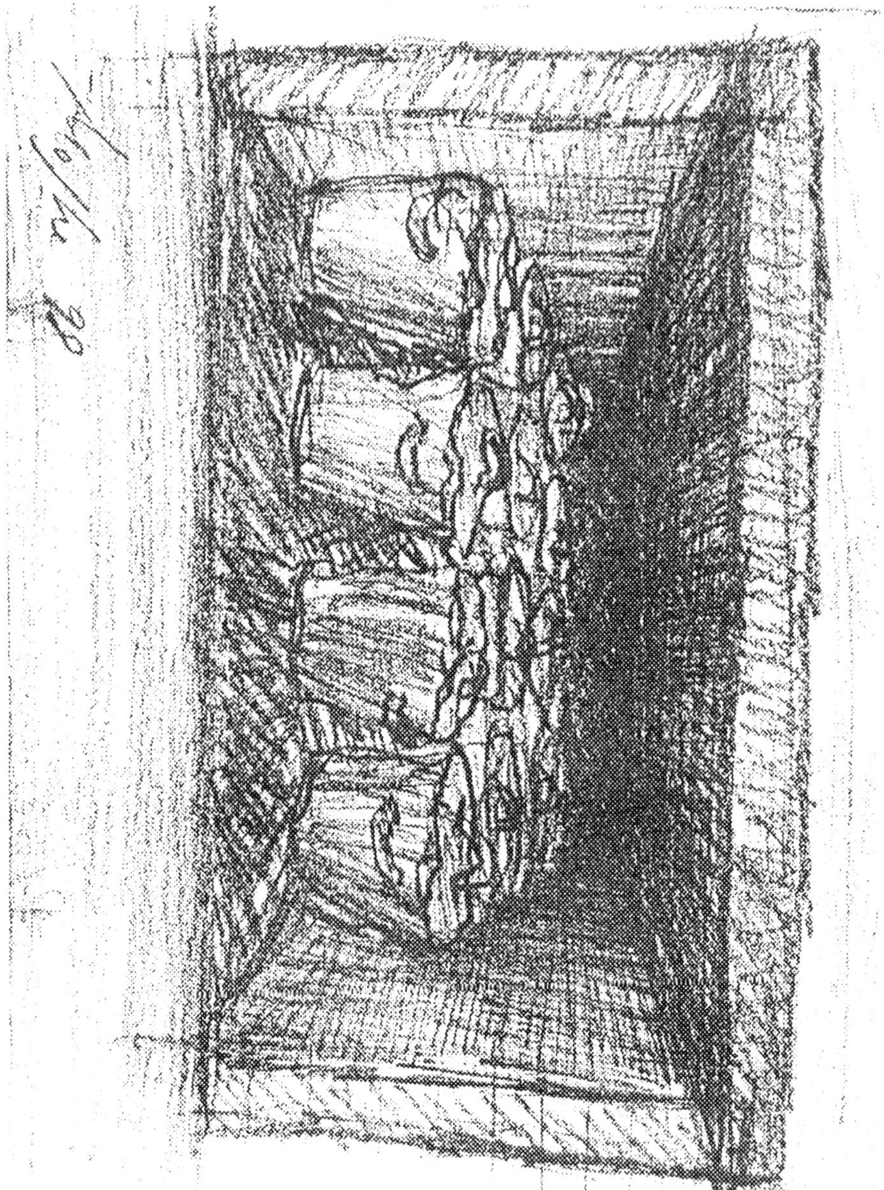

The figure in the bin is a memory of near death

The Wash Room
Towards the back door at the far end was where my hiding place was
Not illustrated in this picture are the containers themselves and where they were placed

18
Out of Auschwitz

I have no idea how long I remained there. I must have fallen asleep. Starvation makes you so week that you can fall asleep in the most improbable circumstances. Hungarian voices and the sound of running water woke me up. This meant that the barracks on the right had now been 'emptied' and the women remaining on the left were allowed out again. I tried to get out of the bin, but I could not. I don't know if I was stuck because the bottom of the bin was very narrow or if my legs were too numb to unfold.

I could not stand up. I tried and tried until the container tipped over with a clatter. Some women came and helped me out. They had heard the commotion the evening before but had not known what it was all about. When I explained what had happened, they told me that my mother was in their barracks. I went in and found her in tears. She had not expected ever to see me again. We cried in each other's arms.

When she heard what I had done to look for her, she realised that the shoe I still had could give me away by being matched with the one I had left behind. She made me hide it in the far corner of the top bunk where no-one was likely to look. She wanted to give me her own shoes but I could not wear them. By then, I was almost as tall as she was and my feet were bigger than hers.

Of course, the barracks I had left to look for my mother was now empty. I had escaped the gas chamber. The following day, I found out that of the 32,000 women who had arrived with us in C lager, only a few hundred were left.

On the morning following the last selection, we were transferred to the B lager. For a brief time, we were able to move freely within the lager. The women there were also Hungarian and surnames were exchanged to locate anyone we knew and to try and find out the fate of relatives and friends.

As people were looking around for their kin, two girls grabbed my hands and said they were Hochhauser girls. They looked to me to be about eighteen or twenty years old, although it was difficult to put an age on the stubbly-haired skeletons that we were. We may well have been cousins as my father's family were scattered through Hungary and I did not know all of them very well. I never met them again and do not remember their first names. They had apparently heard me calling the name Hochhauser when I searched for my mother on that first night in the C lager. News travelled fast among the prisoners and they had also heard that the noise and shouting of the evening before had been due to the Germans searching for a Hochhauser girl. They were glad to see me and my mother still together. Then we said good-bye. We had to go to the gates. We were being transferred to camp Mauthausen, in Austria.

19
Mauthausen

Arriving from Auschwitz, anything would have been an improvement. And in spite of the wretched state we were in, starving and weak, in spite of the way we were treated, we remained human enough to be struck by the beauty of the Austrian mountain landscape. What is more, the air was clear of that terrible smell...There were no wooden barracks, only one long brick building divided in sections. Only the toilets were in a big wooden shed but the lavatories, all in a row, were separated from one another by short partitions. Even though the front remained open, it was a privacy of sorts at last, undreamt of after what we had been through. And it was clean.

We were allotted each a pair of lace-up boots with wooden soles and a uniform which was like a pair of striped pyjamas with a hood, still no underwear. A number was sewn on the front, below the left shoulder. Mine was 623 and my mother's 624.

In Auschwitz, there had been too many of us to be counted one by one and they checked the number of lines, neatly displayed by the supervisors, making sure that there were no gaps in the columns. Here, we did not stand in orderly lines but gathered in a group outside the building for the daily roll-call. We still had no names; we answered 'ja' (yes) when our number was called.

We slept in very long rooms, in which the bunks were arranged in pairs, two up, two down, with one bunk for each person. We each had a sack to lie on, filled with crumpled brown paper, and a thin grey blanket to cover ourselves.

It was winter now. Snow was falling. The water in the washroom was too cold to really clean ourselves. It was as cold inside the washroom as out, which was not helped by a broken window. The place was too small to accommodate us all together so we queued to wash our hands and face and perhaps drink some water.

My mother and I shared a pair of upper bunks . A woman with her young niece, who told me she was sixteen years old,

I was given the number 623 on my uniform, pre-fixed by the letter "U"
"U" stood for the German word "Ungar", meaning Hungarian

had the bunks below us. The girl understood German and reported the soldiers' conversations when she heard them talk among themselves. There were quite a few German women, most of them in uniform, but also some in civilian clothes. One end of the building was given to their offices. Next to the offices were the high gates, set into equally high walls, which would be opened to let us in and out as we were taken to work and back again by a detachment of armed soldiers.

We were sent to work in different places. Some had duties which varied, others worked at the same job every day. We worked day shifts or night shifts as work went on around the clock, the change from one to the other being made from time to time for no apparent reason. We came back each day to return to the same or another assignment the following day. But each day, there were workers who did not return at all. The number of prisoners dwindled rapidly.

20
Slave Labour

I was in a group of about sixty women who went to work at the 'Lenzing Zellwolle AG' factory at a forty-five minutes walk from the camp. The sprawling factory compound included many separate buildings, some of which were linked together by huge metal tubes.

I stood on a turntable with a machine in front of me. A sort of rough, whiteish, wool poured out of one of these giant tubes high up on the wall onto a conveyor belt which brought the stuff to the machine. I would pick up a very big empty bag, put it in place, press a button. The bag would fill up tight with the stuff. I would then press another button, the bag would be tied up, forming a big, heavy bale which disappeared on the conveyor belt. I would pick up another empty bag, place it, press the button, and so on, non-stop. I stood on the turntable, pressing buttons all day or all night, hours at a stretch, every day of every week, endlessly. All this on a ration of thin soup served up at the beginning of the shift into the metal container we had to carry with us at all times, together with our wooden spoon.

I don't know how long the shifts were since we had no way of telling the time. All I can say is that a day shift would begin before dawn and end well after sunset. But at least it was warm in the factory and I did not know then that the heat was due to overworked, unoiled, overheating machinery releasing dangerous fumes. There were cold and warm water taps above a deep, square trough against the wall. We could go to the toilets two by two, escorted by soldiers, at given times when the machines were turned off for the purpose. Then back again to the mind-numbing routine of bag grabbing and button pressing while going round and round on the turntable. And hungry, always hungry.

I was now four months from my thirteenth birthday.

I wished that my mother could be with me. She was much worse off than I was as part of a gang of women who had to shovel snow in the freezing cold.

Photo taken in 1998 - Zellwollen, annexe of Mauthausen

Back in the camp, we did not have to stand still as in the C lager in Auschwitz. We could come and go within the camp grounds. But of course there was no way to leave the compound. On one side were the high walls; on the other a small space between overgrown trees enabled us to see that we must be right on the edge of some expanse of water, either a lake or a river. I learnt later that Mauthausen was a town built on the banks of the Danube, the river of the pleasant weekends of my happy early childhood, which flows through both Hungary and Austria. We could just see the pretty houses right across the water. Life there was going on as usual. Did anyone know about us? The barracks windows were so small that no-one's head could pass through them. Any attempt at escape from the camp was impossible. Still, some of the women desperately tried to find a possible way out.

The girl who spoke German told us that she overheard the soldiers talking among themselves; should we try to run off during the walks to and from work, they would shoot to kill. In any case, each one of the soldiers escorting us as we walked in one line, five abreast, held a German shepherd dog on a lead, so close to us as to almost touch us and these dogs were trained to kill. What is more, once outside the gates, the path we followed was hemmed in by hills on either side.

Apart from an old maintenance man working alone high above a metal bridge, we never saw anyone outside the camp on our way to work and back.

Fifty-Three years later, I discovered by way of the Mauthausen Museum archives that we had to walk to work and back, a brisk 45 minutes each way.

We had no knowledge of time, date or day - only cold and snow, 4 months of winter.

We had only our canvas striped uniforms to keep us warm. We never talked about our work, or conditions.

Only my late mother told me that their group of women was working outside, snow-clearing, without any extra clothing.

21
Thirteenth Birthday

Every few weeks, we would all gather in the courtyard to exchange our dirty striped uniforms for clean ones. Each time we could see that there were less of us. More and more numbers were being left out of the roll-call. I asked the German speaking girl to try and find out from the civilian German women who were handing out the clothes where the missing women had gone. We were told that other camps needed the manpower more, so they had been transferred there. We tried to convince ourselves that wherever they were, their conditions were better than ours, with more and better food, shorter walks to work, shorter working hours... But we knew it was unlikely.

At a short distance, over the hills, we could see trains winding they way round. Someone mentioned that any passengers looking out of the windows could see us. But surrounded as we were by soldiers, we could not even signal. Anyway, what chance was there of anyone coming to get us out of there?

When you are starving, you can think of nothing but food. Whenever we were gathered indoors, the general talk was of food. We talked of the meals we would have one day if we ever got out. We talked of past meals and exchanged recipes. I asked my mother to give the recipes of her cakes which I liked so much. I remember one woman trying to memorise the amount of all the ingredients for each recipe!

One evening we were told that there was to be no work on the following day because it was Christmas. This was the first time that we knew the date and from then on we tried to keep track of time.

Then a day came when my friend's aunt did not return from work. My mother and I tried to comfort her with the usual stories of a camp where she might be better off. But the girl was too upset to get up for work. Surprisingly, she was allowed to stay in for several days.

Then came the terrible day. On the 11th of January, two days before my thirteenth birthday, my mother did not return from work. She and several others in her snow clearing detail were never seen again.

I could not stop crying and I refused to get out of my bunk. Two German women came in and told me that it would be all right for me to stay in. I remained there for two nights and two days before they came back. They handed me a navy blue dress with a white collar and told me that I could go and stay in their office for a few days.

"For your thirteenth birthday treat, Klara".

How did they know? Never did anyone there ever ask for a name or a date of birth. We were just numbers. I puzzled over this and for years I did not know the answer. But of course now we know that even through the horrors of their so-called 'final solution', the ever efficient German SS kept detailed records of everyone and everything.

Inside their office, several women in army uniform were busy writing or sewing, in absolute silence. One section was given to needlecraft. They tried to show me how to make small embroidered doilies, little rag dolls and other such things but I was not interested in anything. I just spent all day holding a small rag doll. Still, for five days I was treated well. The food was better and the women tried to console me by saying that people sent to other camps were better off, did not have to work so hard. Every night I went back to sleep in my bunk . After five days the soldiers came to take me back to work. I was not allowed to keep the doll. I cried all the time.

22
The Living Dead

One of the women among us set herself up as a fortune-teller. In secret, in a corner, she would look at your palm and tell you that one of the lines showed a return journey. And this line met with other lines which indicated the people with whom you would be reunited on your return. She managed to keep us going for a while, with her kind inventions, in a world of make-believe. Until we found out, as was bound to happen, that she told exactly the same story to everyone, to help us keep our spirits up.

Eventually, there were so few of us left that the roll-call was stopped. Only those who were going to work were called. We were all in one room and we were no longer going to work every day. The days became warmer. Once again we lost track of the date. We sat on the ground in the courtyard. The Alsation dogs were nowhere to be seen. There was no more shouting of orders. Only two women were left in the office.

The work stopped altogether. We no longer had the strength to walk. We just sat on the ground outside or lay on our bunks. Of the original few hundreds, twenty or so women were left.

A day came when, having dragged ourselves outside to sit in the open air, we could not see a single soldier or guard. The place seemed deserted. We sat propped up against the wall. One of us suddenly pointed at the gate. It was half open and no-one was guarding it. We were stunned, too weak even to realise that we were now free to walk out. We tried to gather up our thoughts. We did not even know where we were...

Suddenly, the gates open wide. Soldiers are coming in. Not German soldiers. They are... Americans! But just inside the gates, they stop. Some of them even step back. Their faces register deep shock. As they stand there for some time staring at us, we burst into tears. Finally, one of them asks: "Does anyone here understand English?" Yes, one woman does. He explains that they will organise transport to take us somewhere, that we will only have to wait a few minutes. We can see some of the soldiers wiping their eyes. They leave. They have not come near us, only stood there just inside the gates. They seemed almost afraid of us, petrified by the sight we presented, creatures hardly recognisable as women.

23
A Handful Of Survivors

The day was May 6th 1945. The war had ended. A small bus arrived to pick up the few of us who had survived. I wondered how these soldiers had managed to find us. No proper road led to our camp, only a narrow path between the hills, leading to a dead-end surrounded by overgrown bush. The Americans were quick and efficient. In no time at all, a small bus took us to a holiday camp where the first thing that struck me were the flowers. There were flowers everywhere. We never saw the American soldiers again. Red Cross workers took over and within hours we had showered and were wearing proper clothes and shoes.

We were taken aback to learn that this holiday camp had been established for the 'Hitler Youth'. It was one of the training camps where German teenagers were indoctrinated into Nazism. But we did not brood about that. We were too happy to be alive and free, to be sleeping in real beds with bedside tables in a small, pleasant dormitory.

The first food we were given on arrival was a glass of milk. I only managed to drink half of it. My stomach could not take it. We could help ourselves to anything we wanted to eat, but none of us could swallow more than a few mouthfuls. For three days, we just learnt to readjust to the basics of a normal life : keeping clean, sleeping on a mattress with a pillow and, very gradually, taking in food again.

Hungarian survivors had been brought here from other camps as well. Our names and last home addresses were taken so that arrangements could be made for repatriation. Survivors under sixteen years old were the first to be registered. Those who were older could choose not to go back to their place of origin if they so wished. But most people wanted to return to the place they had once called home in the hope of finding some surviving relatives. I was too young to have a choice, but this is what I desperately wanted to do anyway. I believed that all my family would return as I had and that we would all be reunited.

Within a few days, I was with other survivors on a train to Budapest. On arrival, we were taken straight to the Jewish Hospital. Every wing, every ward of the hospital was staffed by Jewish Hungarian-born doctors and medical staff who, having emigrated long ago to America, Britain, or some other parts of the Commonwealth, had escaped Hitler's dragnet over Europe and come back to Budapest in order to help treat Hungarian survivors. The country had been liberated six months before, on December 5th, 1944. By now everything was well organised. Offices had been opened to meet all needs concerning health, lodgings and even employment for those who recovered enough to work.

The hospital kept the Red Cross informed about new arrivals so that families could be reunited. There were also billboards on which we could post the names of the people we were trying to find.

In the hospital, I found myself in a ward for the under sixteen age group. We had a whole building to ourselves. Boys were at one end of the corridor, girls at the other. In the evening, we met in the visitors waiting-room for counselling sessions with the medical staff. They took pains to explain to us that well chosen food needed to be introduced slowly and gradually, in small amounts, in order to heal our swollen tummies. So we duly followed the diet carefully worked out for us at the hospital.

A skin rash over my whole body (only my face was clear) meant that I was covered in cream and bandages, somewhat hidden by the large, roomy pyjamas provided by the hospital.

None of us had any visitors.

24
Margit

One day, to my surprise, I had a visitor. Margit, my grandmother's former housekeeper, had traced me to the hospital. A nurse had to bring her to my bed as she could not recognise me. We both burst into tears. It was the first time I had ever seen her in unfamiliar surroundings and without her white apron. She, for her part, was very upset at the sight of all my bandages. She promised to come again the following day. But she asked the nurses to arrange her visit in a private room and with a doctor present.

She told me that she would only be able to come and see me one more time as she had obtained a job far away and would have to move there into a government-owned home. But she had a lot to tell me before she left Budapest.

On her second visit, she brought me some family photos which she had managed to save and a bar of soap of which there was a great shortage. Then she gave me her news...

Dear Margit had apparently spent the last six months looking at lists of survivors who had either returned to Hungary or gone to other countries. Of our whole family, she had been unable to find anyone besides me - and my father. This is how I found out that I was not completely alone. But good news and bad news came together, since there was no trace of my mother, or little Eva, or anyone else in my family besides my father and myself.

Margit told me that my father was, with many others, in the isolation ward of a hospital, suffering from yellow fever and other ailments. She was not allowed to visit him, but the news had been conveyed to him that I had returned. My hospital staff knew all this, but they had wanted to wait until I was stronger before telling me that, apart from my father and me, my whole family had perished.

I was in a good hospital, well looked after, provided with all I needed and among other young people, some of whom were even worse off than I was as no-one at all in their families had returned. We comforted one another as best we could.

The news of my tremendous loss was so hard to accept that I was crying all the time. I adored my mother and would not accept the fact that she would not come back. I wanted to believe that she was alive, somewhere...I had to be given some tranquilliser. For two whole months I could not stop crying unless I took this medication. The others stayed in bed, too. Still, we were young, and after two months we were all on the way to recovery thanks to the good care and attention we received.

When the day came for us to leave the hospital, doctors and nurses gave us what was thought at the time to be the best possible advice, which I tried to follow until quite recently: "Your new life begins to-day. Forget the past, live in the present and create a future for yourselves. Never look back. Look forward and plan your life step by step."

We know better now. We know that you need to face up to your past and work it out of your system before you can build a mentally healthy future. But psychology had not reached this point yet and our doctors counselled us as best they knew how at the time. Many survivors received the same advice. Could this be the reason why many have waited fifty years and more to tell the story which has weighed them down for so long?

25
Life With Father

My father and I we were due to move together into a small flat allocated to us by the authorities and partly furnished by overseas Jewish organisations, mostly from the United States. But I was released from hospital one month before he was and as the law did not allow a thirteen year old child to live alone, I had to spend the time in a special home for children under sixteen who had no family left or who were still hoping and searching.

I was able to visit my father often during that month. He was still in isolation and we had to speak through a glass partition. The first visit was painful because neither of us could recognise the other.

When I tried to get the medical staff to explain to me the exact nature of my father's illness, all I could get out of them was that he was well on the mend and would soon be home. Home? We had lost our home and with it his workshop which was our livelihood.

My father was badly traumatised. He had lost all at once not only the wife he loved dearly, but also his two brothers and two sisters and their spouses and children. To this was added the anxiety of the dutiful, responsible family man who found himself unable to make a home for his daughter and provide for her.

He did come out of hospital after one month and we moved into the flat assigned to us which we had to share with a childless couple. There were two small bedrooms for us and one for them. This flat had originally been conceived for one family, so sharing it with strangers demanded extreme patience and consideration from all parties.

On the whole, I would say that my state of mind was fairly normal considering what I had been through, although I cried myself to sleep most nights. And sometimes I would see from a distance a woman whom I thought looked like my mother and I would walk up to her. I could not bring myself to believe that the mother I loved so much would not come back, that I would not find her alive. She was so young, only thirty-five years old!

For ten years or so, I went on walking up to people when I thought there was a resemblance with my mother, my little cousin Eva or one of my aunts or uncles.

Unable to deal with my loss, I needed constant medication against depression.

My father had been in Bergen-Belsen which was, like Auschwitz-Birkenau, a combination hard-labour and extermination camp. Even after his release from hospital, he was not well enough to work. Still, he was entitled to have lunch at the 'Joint', an American Jewish organisation where survivors could get a good, free lunch. The place opened between 11 a.m. and 3 p.m. so that every one could avail themselves of the facilities whatever work-shift they were on. The Hungarian government had decreed shift work in order to give employment to as many people as possible. This was the positive side of the communist regime.

26
Picking Up The Pieces

We now lived under a communist regime and we were no longer required by law to state our religion on any document. I was delighted about this as one of the after-effects of my experiences was the wish not to display my Jewish identity. I still feel to-day that one's religious convictions should not have to be registered. Another legacy of my past is the horror of the shaved heads of Auschwitz which made it impossible to recognise your own family in a crowd. I must have long hair. Even to-day, I need to feel the hair on my shoulders and if anyone thinks the style is not right for my age, that is just too bad!

My father was granted a small state pension as the doctors agreed that he needed more time for complete recovery. He never discussed with me or ever spoke in my presence of what had happened to him, nor did he ever ask me any questions about what had happened to my mother and myself since the last time we saw him before we were confined to the ghetto.

As everyone knows, it is only fifty years later that most survivors of the holocaust can finally tell it all. Some of us are following psychologists' advice to unburden ourselves of memories that choke us. Others, like myself, are determined to leave our testimonies in the hope that it may be a deterrent to further genocides. In my case, I find it no easier to speak now than I did fifty-three years ago. The tears still flow whenever I think back. I am still on a permanent course of medication against depression. I am unable to forget my whole family, their faces frozen in time...my mother...my grandmother...my four-year old cousin and her mother...and so many others...thirty people altogether, all too young to die.

I met Susan again, the girl who lived next door to me in the ghetto. She had gone back to Peterzsebet, looking for anyone she knew. She found me living with my father in Budapest. She was alone. Of her whole family in Hungary, she alone had survived. In 1947, she was traced by an uncle from New-York who took her to the U.S.A. where she became a nurse. Then we lost contact with each other - until fifty years later. But this is another story.

27
Communist Hungary

While living in the children's home, I had begun training in a state-owned menswear factory. I was now working there with other young people under twenty-five years old. We worked like robots, at tremendous speed, eight hours a day, six days a week. But there were rewards. Even if the wages were low, the perks were many.

Besides getting cheap tickets for theatres and other outings, we could attend free seminars and classes for numerous activities such as sports, even ice-skating, music, acting and, of course, lectures to learn all about communist ideals. I tried a few of these exercises, but I was more interested in a group of young Jewish survivors who held their meetings in a flat and discussed the possibility of emigrating to Palestine, as it was then called. In everyone's mind was the idea that only a country of our own would ensure no possible recurrence of the persecutions that Jews had endured for centuries, culminating into the horror of the extermination camps. At that time, the Hungarian communist government still allowed people to leave the country in an organised, legal way.

From what we heard of conditions in Palestine, they were a challenge taken by healthy young pioneers, willing and ready to create a country out of a desert. They worked at trying to fertilise arid lands and lived in tents and in the hope of being able to build proper houses one day. However, my father had no-one left but me and I did not want to go anywhere without him. Even though he was slowly getting better, he would not have been strong enough to put up with such harsh conditions, in a very different climate and with limited health care.

He had eventually been given a part-time job in an office where, with others like himself, he could work whatever hours suited him. He therefore had time for his treatments and was also able to meet people of his own age group in 'espresso bars', which were then the popular meeting places.

****

My Father, Age 45, Hungary
His identity card photo that we used to come to England

Klara, Budapest 1948, Age 16
My identity card photo which we had to carry with us at all times

Budapest 1948. With the communist regime tightening its grip, the radio gave no news from outside the communist world, the other side of what the rest of the world called the iron curtain. As for television, there was none in Hungary yet. But my friends who had migrated to Israel kept in touch and from them I received the news that Palestine, which had been under English mandate, had now been divided between the Arabs and the Jews. After 2000 years, we had a country of our own again, called Israel. I brought the news to my father who was moved to tears. Many more youngsters joined the club formed by those who wanted to emigrate to the reborn Jewish state. But it was no longer possible to leave Hungary. The borders were closed.

This is the secret landing at Haifa Shores by Jews, into what was then Palestine. The event was commemorated by all of Israel after 40 years, in 1988

28
The Hungarian Uprising

It is now 1956. I am still working at the menswear factory. My father has another part-time job in a depot where lorries bring fruit and vegetables from farming cooperatives all over the country for re-distribution. He has to deal with red tape and documents a few hours each day. He goes on taking a quantity of tablets daily and he looks well enough.

One day, I am at work as usual when we hear shooting, glass breaking, shouting. It is the beginning of the uprising of the people against the regime. They are tired of low wages, of the endless queues for food and heating fuel, tired of living under the lack of freedom of the communist regime with Russian soldiers everywhere.

We should be working until 10 p.m a.nd it is only 9 p.m., but it is agreed that we should stop work and go home. We find that the tramway is not working, it has been sabotaged. Our flat is in the centre of Budapest and I decide to make my way home on foot as best I can. The streets are full of rubble. All the shops are closed. Shooting is still going on and I seem to be the only person in the street. When I reach home my father is not there.

It appears that young army recruits doing their compulsory two-year military service have broken into and raided an arms depot, taken over the radio station and by evening, they have also taken the newspaper offices of the 'Communist Voice' which is across the road from our flat.

When eventually my father reaches home, he tells me of a plan he has devised to leave the country secretly. Because of the uprising, travelling is controlled even within the country, you have to have a very good reason to move about. In no time at all, Russian tanks are on duty at all roads crossings. Roadblocks manned by Russian soldiers are springing up everywhere, especially at frontier towns. As we talk, the newspaper building across the road comes crashing down to the ground: it has been blown up.

It is my father's job which provides us with a means of escape. He has arranged for a lorry driver to meet us on a side street on the following day. We each take with us a small bag containing food and drink and the family photos that Margit gave me, which are all that remains of our past. We also pack some extra sweaters as it is now November, a bitterly cold month in Hungary where winter begins early.

The big lorry is transporting large crates. The driver explains that the safest way is for us to hide in the centre of the lorry, inside two slatted crates, with others piled on top. Whenever he sees a roadblock ahead, he will shout a warning so that we are not taken by surprise.

We are stopped at two road blocks. Each time, as Russian soldiers open the back of the truck and look at the piled up crates filled with fruit and vegetables, my father and I stop breathing. He knows nothing of my terrifying experience hiding in the food bin in Auschwitz and I try to curb the shaking and keep back the tears as the memories flood back. The soldiers check the driver's documents, then wave him on. My father has prepared the necessary documents for the driver who is taking his cargo to Sopron, a town on the Austrian border. All the information is in Hungarian, as is the driver's identity card. The Russian soldiers do not speak or read Hungarian as even the writing is different from theirs, so I doubt they can make head or tail of the documents. They just let the delivery lorry go through. We continue our journey and my father tries to keep up with his treatment as we go, swallowing tablets every two hours and not feeling too well. He is brooding over the fact that he is losing a home for the second time.

29
Good-bye Hungary

We reached our destination in the evening. The driver who had taken quite a risk for us wished us good luck and left. We found a low-cost bed-and-breakfast place. To my surprise, the inn was jam-packed with people carrying small bags, obviously pretending, like ourselves, to be here for a short visit to some relatives.

We had a visit ourselves, from Russian soldiers armed with machine-guns and asking questions in Russian. Someone was able to translate that they wanted the names and addresses of the relatives we had come to see.

Knowing that they were unlikely to check before morning the non-existent names and addresses we had given them, my father and I retired to try and rest for a few hours as we would need all our strength for the following day. When we crept out of the inn quietly at 4 a.m., without breakfast, we did not wake up anyone. If the two old men at the reception desk were awake, they were probably used to the situation and just played possum.

The long trek in the snow towards the Austrian border had begun. We kept meeting other people along the way and gradually, without a word being spoken, a whole group was formed, walking on in absolute silence. It was a typical Hungarian winter night, bitterly cold, the temperature well below freezing, with a clear sky and full moonlight. We were quite well prepared in padded coats and heavy snow boots.

My father had lived in Sopron when doing his apprenticeship as a smith and he knew the town very well. He was able to lead us through the countryside, away from all habitations. We walked on rough ground, through bush and forest and every time a dry frozen leaf or a twig snapped under our feet, we would shake with apprehension as we knew that Russian soldiers must be patrolling the length of the border between Hungary and Austria.

By the time daylight came, late in the morning of this winter day, we were in no-no man's land. We eventually reached a

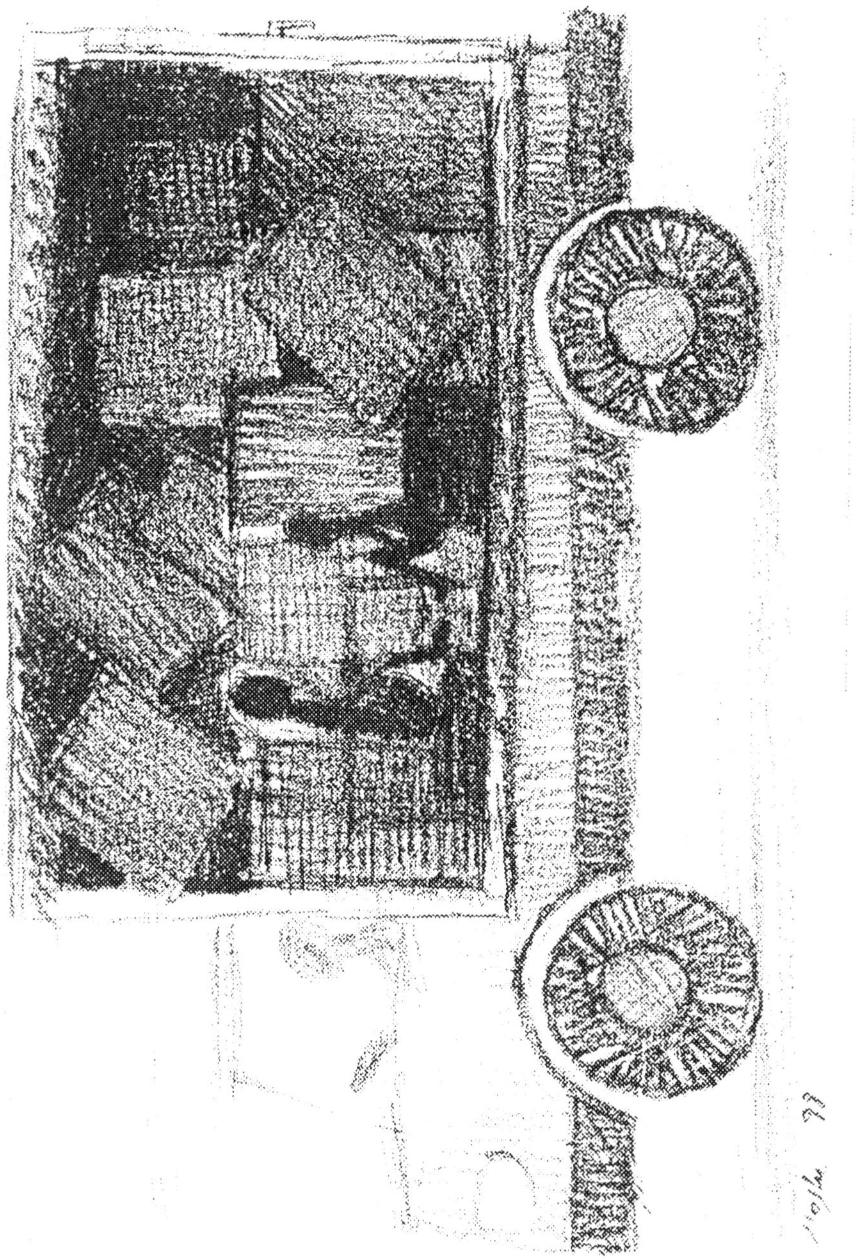

point where a sign indicated land-mines along the road that we had to cross. There was no way of knowing if the sign was just a deterrent, a way to scare people from trying to cross, or if land-mines had indeed been buried there.

My father offered to go first. If he managed to cross safely, we would all follow in his footsteps. He did make it to the other side and, one by one, we crossed the road. Soon after, we reached a patch of grassy land and we all collapsed on the ground. We had walked non-stop for about twenty kilometres. Footwear was not what it is to-day; our feet were swollen, most of us were limping. We were exhausted, but happy. I was back in Austria, this time of my own free will and, hopefully, on my way to somewhere else.

30
Refugees in Vienna

Very cold, but too tired to get up, we enjoyed the beautiful, picturesque scenery with a background of mountains on which patches of snow sparkled on this clear day. But we had to get up and look for signs of human life. As we began to walk again, we saw the road lower down, not too far away. We could even make out the traffic and...yes...cars were parked there, a long line of them, some unmarked and some with the Red Cross sign! They seemed to be waiting for us, as indeed it turned out they were. Many of the vehicles belonged to volunteers who had come with the Red Cross workers to help us out. We had apparently been spotted by low-flying aircraft and the news was on the radio. Because of the Hungarian uprising many people were fleeing into Austria illegally and were rescued and taken in as political refugees from the repressions of the communist regime.

All this was explained to us in English and a young man in our group acted as interpreter. We were taken to a warehouse nearby where hot soup and rolls were being served from a catering van. We were told that we would be driven to Vienna, the capital, where a school had been emptied and desks replaced by camp-beds. This would be our temporary headquarters. Tickets would be handed out for free meals in self-service restaurants. These were the arrangements offered by the Austrian government until we could leave for the country of our choice.

My father and I arrived in Vienna eager to visit this beautiful city which in some ways reminded us of Budapest. However, we were so exhausted that we both needed medical attention. My feet and legs remained swollen for a week after our long march. As for my father, he was very unwell. He was told to continue with his prescription of multiple tablets to be taken with food. He was given a good supply, four containers of each type, altogether sixteen bottles of pills!

We were handed a list of the countries willing to accept a limited number of refugees with the addresses of the various embassies to be approached. Once again, my wish was to go to Israel. My father had doubts. He worried that his state of health would still not allow him to contribute anything valuable to a country in the making and with a much warmer climate than he was used to. But I wanted to try, so we went to make some enquiries.

We spent two weeks site seeing in Vienna. We were quite bowled over by the shops which offered clothes, shoes and food the likes of which we had never seen in Budapest.

Like Budapest, Vienna was built on the banks of the beautiful river Danube and the bridges with their old gas lanterns, which had been retained even though converted to electricity, were fascinating - we crossed the river again and again. We stopped outside restaurants (we could not afford to go in) to listen to the music played inside. We admired the opera house, also from the outside, which reminded us of the one in Budapest.

Most of all I loved the quaint horse-drawn carriages which took people to and from the opera house.

The time came to go to the airport. Until then, I had seen aeroplanes only in newspapers or at the cinema. Both my father and I found the aircraft much bigger than we had expected. At that time, 1956, the BOAC jet was the largest aircraft built. We were both a little nervous at the idea of flying. But once in the air, we enjoyed the flight and even found the meal on board delicious. We were on our way to a new life.

31
England

Landing in England on December 6th, 1956, we found that everything had been beautifully planned and organised to receive us. A coach took us immediately to be registered nearby with the help of an interpreter. It then proceeded to Westgate-on-Sea, near Margate, where we were to remain until mid-January.

We found ourselves in a lovely sea-side house which in the summer served as a bed-and-breakfast holiday home. During the bitterly cold Hungarian winters, everything is covered in snow and ice. I could hardly believe the sights around me, green grass and shrubs in December!

We were about twenty refugees in this house and only one young man among us could speak English. Yet local families invited us into their homes for Christmas lunch. They even had small gifts for us in Christmas stockings . My father was feeling a great deal better as he could spend his time resting. We loved the colourful lights strung up over the streets and the cheerfulness around us. Everything was new and wonderful to us. We had never seen anything like this in Hungary.

Not only the Christmas celebrations , but the sea was a new experience, too. We enjoyed the sound of the ocean which could be heard from the house, even with the windows closed. Hungary is a land-locked nation, with lake Balaton as its largest expanse of water.

For the first time since my ordeal had begun, I felt a great sense of relief. I no longer had fears of further upheavals. I was truly free. Life was beginning for the third time...

While we rested and recovered and enjoyed ourselves, news was coming every day from London concerning work permits, jobs and accommodation. Everything was being processed swiftly and efficiently. We learnt that my father and I would be allocated rooms at walking distance from each other in North London.

I had a job lined up in a dress factory. Before moving into his bedsitter, my father would have to go to University College

Hospital as an in-patient for a thorough check-up. He was to remain there six weeks. We had no English at all, but that problem had also been temporarily solved. A three-way telephone link-up had been set up with an interpreter so that the hospital staff could speak to me about my father whenever necessary.

32
London

We left Westgate-on-sea in mid-January 1957, looking forward to starting work and seeing my room in a bedsit in North Finchley. Everything had been arranged for us.

We had seen a film in Budapest once, it was called "Waterloo Bridge" and was set in London immediately after the war. It was a very emotional story - soldiers returning after the war - not all their loved ones were waiting for them at the station. All the older generation amongst us had seen the film and for me arriving at Waterloo station this was a moment of high excitement.

But, my expectations turned to disappointment. Smoke from the moving locomotive made the atmosphere dark, the walls were blackened, and a cold draft was blowing.

It was 11.30am. My first glance outside the station was not reassuring: it was dark, drizzling and foggy. The London fog in those days was much more frequent and also much thicker.

But organisation was still top-class. We were taken to our various new flats or bed-sitters by several different interpreters, Hungarians who had moved to England before us, also acting as guides.

The following morning, someone was there to take me to work, to explain the transports system and how the money worked. The currency of the time, consisting of pounds, shillings and pence was not an easy concept to grasp for someone accustomed to the decimal system.

At first, not knowing the language made life complicated. I would go about with an address written on a piece of paper to show my destination. And my landlady in North Finchley only spoke English. But to my surprise we all learnt the ways of things as well as the language in quite a short time. My father was given a dictionary and kind people in the hospital helped him to learn.

They were volunteer workers, Hungarians who had come to London soon after the end of the war. He was found well enough

The London Fog

to be discharged from the hospital but not well enough to work and he was granted unemployment benefit instead of a job.

In a few short months I had to learn English currency; it was twelve pence to one shilling; 20 shillings made one pound; two bob meant two shillings; half a crown was 2 shillings and sixpence; One pound one shilling was called a Guinea! The current decimal system did not come into force until 1969.

But soon we learned, and to speak the language! Of course, my accented English remained, but I began to feel I belonged here.

I was working five and a half days a week and not earning very much, but I soon learnt where I could get the best prices for everything I needed. One of my colleagues at work took me to a market where prices were so reasonable that I even bought - great luxury - a radio. But it took me a long time to understand the programmes!

Teddy-boys were then setting a certain fashion trend : long jackets, drain-pipe trousers, royal blue crepe-sole shoes. The girls wore lacy, gathered underskirts and shoes with stiletto hills and very pointed toes. They danced to rock-and-roll music. I had missed the normal life of a teenager and I very much wanted to have clothes like theirs. Ladies hairstyles became very high and back-combed, all kept in place with hair lacquer. I bought my father a pair of crepe-sole blue suede shoes and he was very happy with them. We both began to feel fashionable. It was something we could not have dreamt of until now, a symbol of our new lives.

Rock-and-rollers of 1956. The boy is in a typical Teddy Boy outfit and the girl is wearing a very full dirndl-type skirt and plain V necked top. Her hair is tied back in a pony tail

33
Alone

For the next six months I went on working and eventually moved to a better bed-sitter, above a restaurant owned by a Hungarian couple. They took us to the cinema and helped us to learn English. I believed that my father's health was continuing to improve. He himself seemed to think that he was on the mend. But in June of that year, one of his neighbours called me to say that he was unwell and that I should come at once. I called an ambulance which took him to the University College Hospital once again.

There I was told that all they could do was to change his medication. His experiences during the war, the suffering both physical and mental which he had endured and the memory of all he had lost, all this affected him very deeply and was playing havoc with his health.

What exactly he went through during those years, I will never know. I found out at the hospital that on his arrival there in January, my father revealed through an interpreter that he knew the fate of everyone in our family. In 1945, while he was hospitalised in Budapest, some Red Cross officials gave him a report on every name he had put forward : there was a document for each name. But before he came out of that hospital, he destroyed and threw away all the papers because he did not want me to see them.

I went to see him at University College Hospital every evening after work. A few days after his admission, a nurse stopped me as I arrived and asked me to go with her into an office where another nurse was waiting. I was asked to sit down, given a glass of water. They tried to tell me the bad news as gently as they could. There was one small bag of my father's belongings to take with me. He was 56 years old.

I thought then that I would never find out the fate that befell any of my relatives. They would tell me nothing here at the hospital, respecting my father's wishes.

34
Marriage Drama

I met Shandor, a young man who, like me, had left Hungary during the uprising of December 1956, and we were married. We had a one year lease on a big furnished house in North London which we shared with other Hungarian immigrants, all under thirty years old. I was the only Jew in the group, but we never spoke of religion or politics. We were all busy learning English and the British way of life. I never questioned anyone about their past and no-one ever asked about mine.

These young people, myself and my husband included, lived as though we had just been born. For each one of us, life had just begun, the past did not exist. I, for one, was determined only to look ahead.

We shared a living-room with a television which was a novelty and a great joy for us all. The whistling kettle was a wonder. Fish and chips shops were then to be found at every corner, long before other fast-foods came out, cheap and jolly and making cooking unnecessary. In fact, fish and chips became our staple diet. Not having to cook, we had more time to enjoy life after working hours.

We would go to the cinema or walk and discover London. We found window-shopping a fascinating pastime as goods had never been displayed in Hungary - you had to go into the stores and ask if they stocked what you wanted. I had let my hair grow long and I found that by becoming a hairdresser's model in a hairdressing school, I could have it done twice a week free of charge.

Among the young people in the house was another married couple, Laslo and Katie. Laslo had bought a motorcycle and often took one of us for a ride. One very foggy morning, Laslo and Shandor left to go riding together. A few hours later, a policeman was at the door to tell Katie and me that our husbands had been involved in a multiple vehicle crash pile-up on the North Circular Road and were both seriously hurt.

I was expecting my first child and so was Katie. For several weeks, we went together to the hospital to visit our husbands.

Shandor and Laslo had each undergone several hours of surgery but remained in a coma. Neither of them ever recovered consciousness.

I was a widow at twenty-six and my son Alexander, born on December 4th 1958, had no father. At the time, there was no help for single mothers and I had no family anywhere to turn to for help.

To find furnished accommodation with a baby was near impossible. Children were not allowed in the house we had shared and in any case the lease was only for one year and was running out.

I eventually found a furnished room in which I managed to live on my meagre social security payment for the first two years of my baby's life. In the end, I had no choice but to place my son in a residential nursery so that I could go to work. I found a job as a waitress. I worked six days a week for minimal wages and could only see Alex once a week.

35
Another New Start

In 1963, I married again, this time an Englishman, Michael Parker. Alex was already five years old and it was wonderful to have him live with me again and to be able to make a home for him.

After eighteen years, I was still unable to come to terms with the fact that being recognised as a Jew was the source of all my troubles and I saw my new name and status as a means of blending in. I now had an English name. Klara was no more: I had become Clare Parker.

But for my new parents-in-law, I was a whole new experience. They had never before come across a foreigner, or even a Jew, English or not, and their son had managed to combine both in his choice of a wife. Needless to say, they did not approve! However, as they lived nearby, they came to see us often and quite soon came to like me enough to confide in me. They even began to complain to me about their son's behaviour and about the great worry he was to them. This was a true sign that I had become a member of the family!

My husband was training to be a shoe-shop manager so that we could obtain the flat above the store, which went with the job. He never told me that the job was in fact that of 'relief manager', which meant that he would have to go from one retail outlet to another all over the country wherever and whenever supervising was needed. When I thought I had achieved stability, we began to move from city to city.

My daughter Anita was born in 1969. Alex was now almost ten years old. Right from the start, Michael and I were having many problems. He was never at home and always left me short of cash. He would disappear on evenings and at week-ends, usually blaming his absences on having to do stocktaking during the store's closing hours.

When I found out that he was cheating on me by dating young girls as well as stealing from his employers to entertain his dates, I tried to have it out with him. His reaction was to hit me.

We were then living in Birmingham. I went to my doctor who referred me to a social worker and I was lucky enough to meet Ruth Wolf. I was not to know until much later that this lovely, modest lady had received an OBE for her work with Holocaust survivors. All I saw was a kind, elderly Jewish lady who had once worked for the Red Cross and had all the necessary knowledge and connections to find me an empty house within a week. She even filled it with all the necessary furniture and appliances for the children and me, from second-hand stores and people she knew.

It was 1972. I began my life as a single mother with fourteen year old Alex and 3 year old Anita. It was better this way for the three of us than life with a dishonest, abusive man. When, in 1974, Alex went to Israel to work as a volunteer in a kibbutz for one year, I took in clothes alterations and repairs so that I could stay at home with my daughter.

Ruth Wolf had retired by then, but she never stopped her regular visits and I greatly benefited over the years from her understanding and advice. Although she had made discreet offers for me to unburden myself to her, stressing that everything I told her would remain confidential, I had never spoken to her of my past, never even mentioned that I was Jewish. But of course she must have sensed it and when I sent my daughter to a Jewish school, Ruth asked me what had happened to me during the war. I had never been able to talk about it to anyone. I started to shake and cry. She sent for my doctor, a Jew from Slovakia who had fought in the British army during the war. Understanding the basic reason for my nervous state, he prescribed tranquilliser tablets.

Ruth Wolf eventually mentioned that if I ever wanted to obtain official documents relating to my family or myself in the camps, she could help me fill out the necessary forms handed out by the Red Cross for the International Tracing Service in Geneva.

I had never really accepted the idea of my mother's death and if there was a chance of finding out what had happened to her, I had to take it. I filled and sent out forms concerning her and myself although I found it hard to understand that there could be any records of people who had never been asked for their names or anything else while they were being processed for slaughter.

A few months later, in January 1977, after thirty-two years, I received the shocking document about my mother, an incomprehensible statement of the accidental death of 'prisoner 624, Magda Hochhauser, nee Goldfinger, deceased on 11th January 1945 at 7a.m. in Concentration Camp Mauthausen/Commando Lenzing. Cause of death: work accident (run over by a train while crossing the railway embankment).'

Even after all this time, the shock was severe. I had no choice now but to admit the finality of the news which I had refused to accept for so long. I did not know then that it would take another twenty years before I found out what had really happened on the fateful day.

The same year, I obtained a divorce from Michael . He married again soon after. We have no contact.

Lőlas Nándor
Lőlas Sándor
Holczer Béla
Holczer Benedit
Holczer Emil
Holczer Ezra
Holczer Gizella
Holczer György
Holczer Henrik
Holczer Imre
Holczer Jenő
Holczer József
Holczer László
Holczer Péter

Hochhauser Gyula
Hochhauser György
Hochhauser Imre
Hochhauser Irvin
Hochhauser József
Hochhauser László
Hochhauser Sándor
Hochmann Benjamin
Hochmann Dezső
Hochmann Emil
Hochmann Gábor

My father's side of the family, Uncle's & Cousins - from the Mouthausen Memorial

SERVICE INTERNATIONAL DE RECHERCHES
INTERNATIONAL TRACING SERVICE
INTERNATIONALER SUCHDIENST

D - 3548 AROLSEN

Tel. (05691) 637 — Telegr.-Adr. ITS Arolsen

EXTRAIT DE DOCUMENTS	EXCERPT FROM DOCUMENTS	DOKUMENTEN-AUSZUG

Votre Réf. / Your Ref. / Ihr Az.: L/EUR/78,025 file 56,924

Notre Réf. / Our Ref. / Unser Az.: T/D - 109 178 -------

Nom / Name / Name: HOCHHAUSER née GOLDFINGER -------

Prénoms / First names / Vornamen: Magda -------

Nationalité / Nationality / Staatsangehörigkeit: Hungarian -------

Date of birth / Geburtsdatum: 11.4.1909 -------

Lieu de naissance / Place of birth / Geburtsort: Budapest -------

Profession / Beruf: housekeeper -------

Noms des parents / Parents' names / Namen der Eltern: not indicated -------

Religion: Jewish -------

Dernière adresse connue / Last permanent residence / Zuletzt bekannter ständiger Wohnsitz: Pesterzsebet

Arrêté le / Arrested on / Verhaftet am: not indicated -------
A In In: not indicated -------

No. de détenu / Prisoner's No. / Häftlingsnummer: not indicated -------
par by durch: not indicated -------

Est entré au camp de concentration / Entered concentration camp / Wurde eingeliefert in das Konz.-Lager: Auschwitz -------

venant de / coming from / von: not indicated -------

le / on / am: not indicated -------

par by durch: not indicated -------

Catégorie, ou raison donnée pour l'incarcération / Category, or reason given for incarceration / Kategorie, oder Grund für die Inhaftierung: "Jüd." (= Jüdin) -------

Transféré / Transferred: on 3rd November 1944 to Concentration Camp Mauthausen/Commando Lenzing,

Deceased on 11th January 1945 at 7.00 in Concentration Camp Mauthausen/Commando Lenzing. Cause of death: work accident (run over by a train while crossing the railway embankment). --------------------

Dernière mention dans la documentation des CC
Last entity In CC records
Letzte Eintragung In KL-Unterlagen

Remarques
Remarks   none --------------------
Bemerkungen

Documents consultés: "Schreibstubenkarte, Zugangsbuch" and "Totenbuch" of Concentration
Records consulted
Geprüfte Unterlagen Camp Mauthausen. --------------------

Expédié à
Dispatched to   HIAS   Arolsen, 7th January 1977
Abgesandt an   European Headquarters
                CH-1211 Geneva 13

A. de COCATRIX
Directeur

Chef des Archives

* A titre explicatif: ce complément ne figure pas sur les documents originaux
* Added by the I.T.S. as explanation, does not appear on the original documents.
* Erklärung des I.T.S. erscheint nicht In den Originalunterlagen.

I received this document 32 years late, in 1977. It looked to me as if my mother had committed suicide

SERVICE INTERNATIONAL DE RECHERCHES
INTERNATIONAL TRACING SERVICE
INTERNATIONALER SUCHDIENST

D - 3548 AROLSEN

Tel (05691) 031 - Telegr Adr ITS Arolsen

| EXTRAIT DE DOCUMENTS | EXCERPT FROM DOCUMENTS | DOKUMENTEN-AUSZUG |

Votre Réf / Your Ref / Ihr Az: L/EUR/78.025 file 56,924

Notre Réf / Our Ref / Unser Az: T/D - 109 179

Nom / Name: HOCHHAUSER
Prénom / First name / Vorname: Klara
Nationalité / Nationality / Staatsangehörigkeit: Hungarian

Date de naissance / Date of birth / Geburtsdatum: 13.1.1932
Lieu de naissance / Place of birth / Geburtsort: Budapest
Profession / Beruf: not indicated

Noms des parents / Parents names / Namen der Eltern: not indicated
Religion: Jewish

Dernière adresse connue / Last permanent residence / Zuletzt bekannter ständiger Wohnsitz: Pestersebet

Arrêté le / Arrested on / Verhaftet am: not indicated
à / in: not indicated
par / by / durch: not indicated

Entrée au camp de concentration / Entered concentration camp / Wurde eingeliefert in das Konz.-Lager: Auschwitz
No de détenu / Prisoner's No / Häftlingsnummer: not indicated
par / by / durch: not indicated

Is not indicated
venant de / coming from / von: not indicated
on / am:

Catégorie ou raison donnée pour l'incarcération / Category, or reason given for incarceration / Kategorie, oder Grund für die Inhaftierung: "Jüdin"

Transféré / Transferred / Überstellt: on 3rd November 1944 to Concentration Camp Mauthausen/Commando Leipzig, Prisoner's No. 623.

Remarques / Remarks / Bemerkungen: **none**

Documents consulted / Records consulted / Geprüfte Unterlagen: cc Liberated on 6th May 1945 by the US-Army in Concentration Camp Mauthausen/Commando Ebensee. "Schreibstubenkarte, Nummernkarte, Zugangsbuch" and "Befreiungs-liste" of Concentration Camp Mauthausen.

Etablie à / Dispatched to / Abgesandt an: IIIAS
European Headquarters
CH-1211 Geneva 13

Arolsen, 7th January 1977

A. de COCATRIX
Directeur

A. ORTIZ
Chef des Archives

- A little erolisctit ce compliment se figure pas sur les documents originaux
- Added by the I.T.S. as explanation, does not appear on the original documents
- — — — — — — — — — — — — — — — — — nicht in den Originalunterlagen

|1or/H/bl|
|Mai 71|

My own document

36
A New Generation

When Anita was seventeen, in the Summer of 1988, it was her turn to go to Israel for six weeks as a volunteer worker. She went to kibbutz Usha, near Haifa. From there she wrote to me that even though the six day week was hard work, she liked the communal life and wanted to take time off from her studies to remain there for a whole year. She enjoyed the company of other young people all the more than we had no relatives and it had always been just the three of us. The kibbutzniks were like one big family, sharing everything, enjoying outings and visits to historic sites together. She loved it all.

Now that I lived alone, I was able to start saving money from my small income so that the following year, in 1989, while Anita was still at Kibbutz Usha, I managed to join a group of volunteers aged forty and over on a working visit to Israel, even though we had to pay our own fare. We worked in a geriatric hospital in Jaffa which provided us with food and shared accommodation.

From Friday after lunch until Sunday morning our weekends were free so at the first opportunity I went to meet Anita at the Haifa central bus station, after one long year. We sat in a coffee-bar for a heart-to-heart talk. She had no intention of ever going back to live in Birmingham. She had quite made up her mind to remain in Israel for good.

Eventually, Anita met a nice young man in the kibbutz, B'rak Gabay, and they were married. She is now an Israeli citizen. Of course, I went back to Israel for the wedding. Everyone in the kibbutz, including the children, took part in planning and organising the wedding. Tables and chairs were borrowed from another kibbutz and set on the wide lawn. Lights were strung up overhead, a beautiful cake was baked in the communal kitchen and I made the bride's dress myself. Everything was provided free of charge in their spare time by these wonderful people in a true community spirit, while work was going on as usual in the daytime.

Alexander, aged 19
In Israel on a year's voluntary work

Anita and Barak in Kibbutz Usha
Israel, 1992

Udi - Age 3
Oren - 7 months

On the 29th of March 1996, my grandson Ehud was born. We call him Udi. How I wish that my parents could see him!

It hurts me to think that my mother will never know she has a grand-daughter who is an Israeli citizen. It hurts me that she will never know that Jews now sing the Hatikvah, not in secret, but proudly as their National Anthem.

I am back in North London where I first lived when I arrived from Hungary. I have a pretty flat in a big old house in which most of the tenants are former refugees who fled from various European countries ahead of Hitler's Gestapo .

Now retired, my time is my own and I have become a member of the Holocaust Survivors' Centre, a social club where I can take part in various activities and enjoy some hobbies I had no time to pursue while working. There, at last, we can talk about our past and unburden our minds. Having suffered similar fates, we understand one another.

On October 22nd 1998, my granddaughter, Oren, was born.

ARBITRARY DEATH

Thus our days proceeded until a terrible accident happened on the 11th January 1945.

As usual at that time we went to work in the dark. On the way between Pettinghofen and Lenzing we had to cross the unguarded railway track. There was much snow on the way and, already in the distance a loudly whistling train could be heard. I marched in a row of five, more at the end of the line.

The train came form the left side towards us. With call such as "everybody must pass the railway truck before the train comes." and "the line must not be broken". The guards urged the line to an even higher speed. However, the guards that marched at the rear of the line probably realised that this was barely possible. The shouted "stop!", which some, who heard and understood, followed up. I myself passed the railway truck by running across. Suddenly, we heard a terrible scream. We were stopped and had to stand for a long time. Then we were taken to a barracks at the factory. There the colleagues began to whisper that someone had been killed by the train.

When we returned to the camp late in the evening my sister, who worked in the sick bay, was waiting for me, her eyes frighteningly glaring, she was out of her mind. She had heard that the train had killed five girls. After hearing this information, broken bones and mutilated bodies, still soaked in blood had been brought into the camp. Forty Seven years later my sister confessed to me that she thought she had seen amongst the mutilated bodies an (amputated) foot, wearing my shoe. So, until the evening my sister had expected that I was also one of the casualties and when she saw me alive she was at the same time shocked and thrilled with pleasure.

My friend, who on that day felt ill and was permitted to stay in the camp, volunteered to help with the injured when, a short time after the working party had left, it became known about the accident. She did not know what had happened. The helping group took a large sledge in which they collected the mutilated bodies and brought them into the camp. Later they were put in coffins which had been provided. The identity as well as the nationality of the killed girls remained unknown to us.

This piece was translated from German in 1998 from material held in the Mauthausen Museum archives

The Song

You can sing the Yiddishe Mama song
If your mother lived to grow old.
My mother was murdered in the Holocaust
There was no white hair to be seen
When they shaved her head in Auschwitz
She was a young women of thirty-five.
Remembering only breaks my heart
There are wounds that time cannot heal

Klara Parker